A Primer on
TECHNOLOGY
LICENSING

• Kent Press •
Stamford, Connecticut

A Primer on
TECHNOLOGY
LICENSING

GREGORY J. BATTERSBY AND CHARLES W. GRIMES

Copyright © 1996 Kent Communications, Ltd.
All Rights Reserved.
Printed in the U.S.A.

Kent Communications, Ltd.
P.O. Box 1169
Stamford, CT 06904-1169

Publisher's Cataloging in Publication
(Prepared by Quality Books Inc.)

Battersby Gregory J.
A primer on technology licensing / Gregory J.
Battersby, Charles W. Grimes.
p.cm.
Includes index.
ISBN: 1-888206-06-3 (hc)
ISBN: 1-888206-07-1 (pbk)

1. License agreements. 2. Technology transfer--Law
and legislation. I. Grimes, Charles W. II. Title.
K1528.B38 1996   346.7304'8
                              QBI96-20394

*To Susan and Gwynne
without whose love, understanding
and support life would be meaningless.*

About the Authors

Gregory J. Battersby holds an A.B. degree (in biology and chemistry) from Seton Hall University and a J.D. degree from Fordham University School of Law. He is a member of the New York and Connecticut Bars and is admitted to practice as a patent attorney before the United States Patent and Trademark Office. Charles W. Grimes holds a B.S. degree from Pennsylvania State University and a J.D. degree from the University of Denver School of Law. He is a member of the Illinois, New York and Connecticut Bars and is admitted to practice as a patent attorney before the United States Patent and Trademark Office.

Messrs. Battersby and Grimes are co-founding partners of the Stamford, Connecticut intellectual property law firm of Grimes & Battersby, Three Landmark Square, Stamford, CT 06901 (203) 324-2828 which specializes in patents, trademarks, copyrights, unfair competition, antitrust and corporate law and licensing, with a particular emphasis on the merchandising, multimedia, entertainment, edutainment, toy, animation and publishing industries. They have authored **The Law of Merchandise and Character Licensing, Licensing Law Handbook 1985, Multimedia and Technology Licensing Agreements: Forms and Commentary, The Essential Guide to Merchandising Forms** and **The Toy & Game Inventor's Guide, Second Edition**. They serve as Executive Editors of *The Licensing Journal* and *The IP Litigator* and Editors in Chief of the *Multimedia & Technology Licensing Law Report*.

Mr. Battersby is currently the Treasurer of the New York Intellectual Property Law Association (NYIPLA) and for many years has been editor of the NYIPLA *Bulletin*, **Greenbook** and **Annual**. He is a guest lecturer at the Franklin Pierce Law School Advanced Licensing Institute. Mr. Grimes is an Adjunct Professor at Sacred Heart University where he teaches intellectual property law and has served on the Editorial Board of *The Trademark Reporter*. They frequently lecture and write on a variety of intellectual property matters.

Preface

The licensing of intellectual property rights is big business. Virtually every day, we read about how Texas Instruments or IBM adds billions of dollars to their bottom line from the royalty income they receive from the licensing out of their patents and technology. Similarly, we see virtual start-up companies flourish and grow on the strength of the technology licenses they take from others.

The purpose of this book is to explain the basics of patent and technology licensing and, specifically, the why's and wherefore's of the licensing process. As attorneys who work in the licensing field, we are asked daily by clients to explain how the process works. We regularly hear questions like:
- Why should I consider letting another use my technology or patents?
- How do I go about getting started?
- Does the technology have to be patented and, if so, will it command a higher royalty rate?
- How should I price my technology (or, conversely, how much should I pay to use another's patent)?
- What should I look out for in a license agreement?
- Is it legal?
- Can I license my technology outside the United States and, if so, how do I go about doing it?
- What are the risks attendant to entering into a licensing program?

In this book, we have tried to answer these and other fundamental questions. We intend this work to serve as a basic resource guide for those contemplating a jump into the licensing arena as well as for the junior licensing executive or licensing attorney who seeks answers to those never ending questions. We even suspect that the senior licensing counsel or licensing executive might find some pearls of wisdom buried throughout its pages, although we don't expect that they will ever admit it.

In organizing this book, we attempted to simulate the steps of a traditional licensing program, i.e., making the decision to license in or out; identifying and protecting the licensing properties; putting a value on the properties; seeking out potential licensees; negotiating the license agreement and administering the program. Recognizing that many of our readers will be unfamiliar with the "lingo" of licensing, we tried to define along the way the commonly used terms. In addition, being intellectual property attorneys, we felt that an "Intellectual Property Law 101" discussion was appropriate.

Recognizing that licensing is global in nature, we also considered the aspects of international licensing. In recent years, there has been a growing concern over the monopolistic powers of licensing and, accordingly, we decided to include a chapter on antitrust issues. We closed the work with specific issues involved in the multimedia and biotechnology licensing industries.

Last, but not least, we packed the appendix with legal forms. We even provided an annotated form of the basic license agreement to assist readers in understanding the document on a point-by-point basis.

A preface would not be complete without an expression of our appreciation for the contributions of certain individuals who assisted us in the preparation of this book. Special thanks must be extended to our former associate and friend, David Sigalow, who tired long and hard between court sessions to assist us in the preparation of the original manuscript. Similarly, we are indebted to Russell Parr for his contribution in the valuation chapter. Russell is a recognized expert on the valuation of intellectual property, and we believe that this chapter greatly enhanced this work. The reader will also benefit from Craig Blakeley's section on multimedia licensing, which is a very informative treatment of a subject everyone is talking about, but few seem to understand. We thank him for preparing that section. Our associate, Jim Coplit, also proved invaluable in compiling the appendix and in overall editing.

Last, but by no means least, are Michelle Lostaglio and Katie DeVito of our publisher, Kent Press. Their day-to-day assistance, prodding and editing made this work a reality. These two young ladies are very special and the reason why Kent Press is rapidly becoming *the* publishing house for licensing matters.

GJB and CWG

Table of Contents

One: The Why's and Wherefore's of Licensing   *1*
   Licensing Benefits: The Licensor's Perspective *2*
   Licensing Benefits: The Licensee's Perspective *4*
   Licensing In vs. Licensing Out   *5*
   What Are the Risks?   *6*

Two: Getting Started   *9*
   Licensing Out *9*
     Sources of Licensable Technology *10*
     Setting Up the Framework *12*
     Creating a Marketing Plan *13*
     The Role of a Consultant or Agent *14*
     The Lawyer is Your Friend *15*
     Finding the Right Licensees *16*
   Licensing In *17*
     Identifying a Need *18*
     Locating Compatible Technology or Patents *19*
     Approaching the Property Owner *20*

Three: The Basics of Intellectual Property Law   *23*
   Intellectual Property Law "101" *23*
   Patents *26*
     No Protection During the Patent Pending Stage *27*
     The Patent Process *27*
   Trademarks *29*
   Copyrights *32*
   Unfair Competition *35*
   Other Forms of Intellectual Property Protection *36*
   Overlapping Forms of Protection *37*
   Legal Notices *39*
   International Protection *40*

Four: Valuing Patents and Technology for Licensing   *43*
by Russell L. Parr
   Going Beyond Commodity Earnings *48*

Market Approach *51*
The Scarcity of Market Data *54*
Comparability *56*
Royalty Rate Determination Methods *61*
Market Transactions In General And On Average *61*
Rules-of-Thumb that Don't Work *64*
    The "25%" Rule *65*
    The Industry Norms Method *67*
    The Return on R&D Costs Method *68*
    The Return on Sales Method *69*
    The 5% of Sales Method *69*
Complex Factors That Can Impact Royalty Rates *70*
Infringement Damages Analysis *71*
Infringement Damages: The Analytical Approach *72*
Normal Industry Profits *74*
A More Comprehensive Analytical Approach *74*
Failure of The Analytical Approach *77*
Infringement Damages: Qualitative Factors *77*
Considering the *Georgia Pacific* Factors *80*
Summary *82*

Five: Negotiating License Agreements   85

Drafting the Licensing Memorandum *88*
The Confidential Disclosure Agreement *90*
Making an Oral Presentation *93*
The Evaluation Process *95*
Option Agreements *97*

Six: The License Agreement   101

The Letter of Intent *103*
The Battle of Forms *106*
Terminology *107*
Grant of Rights *109*
Compensation *110*
Accounting and Royalty Investigations *113*
Improvements and Grant Backs *115*
Intellectual Property Responsibilities *116*
"Favored Nations" Clauses *118*
Representations, Warranties and Indemnification *118*
Termination *119*

Governing Law and Disputes *121*
Assignability and Sublicensing *122*
Integration *123*

Seven: Antitrust Considerations   125
The Basics of U.S. Antitrust Law *125*
The Microsoft Example *128*
The New Antitrust Guidelines *130*
Patent Misuse and Technology Licensing *132*

Eight: International Licensing   137
Foreign Export Controls *137*
Protection of Intellectual Property
and Trade Secrets *142*
Local Regulations *145*
Currency *146*
Licensing in the European Community *149*
Licensing in the Pacific Rim *153*
    Japan *154*
    People's Republic of China *156*
    South Korea *159*

Nine: Administering the Licensing Program   163
Accountability *165*
Determining Whether a Problem Exists *165*
Royalty Investigations Explained *166*
The Royalty Investigation *169*
What the Investigation May Reveal *170*
Whether or Not to Investigate *173*

Ten: Special Forms of Licensing   177
Biotechnology *177*
    The Biotech Alliances of Today
    and Tomorrow *178*
    Creative Compensation Structures *180*
    Royalty Determinations *181*
    Enforcing the Intellectual Property Rights *182*
    International Considerations *184*

Multimedia
by Craig Blakeley *185*
   Multimedia Defined *185*
   Multimedia in the Computer Industry *186*
   Interactive Multimedia *187*
   "Virtual Reality" *188*
   Legal Issues *189*
   Conclusion *190*

Appendices   *193*
   List of Resources *193*
   List of Technology Management Consultants *196*
   Sample Confidential Disclosure Agreement *203*
   Sample Consulting Agreement for the
   Technical Consultant *209*
   Sample Option Agreement *219*
   Sample Patent License Agreement
   with Annotations *221*
   Sample Technology License Agreement *252*
   Sample Multimedia License Agreement *268*

Index   *287*

ONE:
The Why's and Wherefore's of Licensing

For the purposes of this book, the working definition for licensing is a situation where an owner (the "licensor") of an intellectual property right (the "licensed property") grants to another party (the "licensee") formal permission to use the owner's intellectual property, subject to certain terms and conditions and typically in exchange for some financial remuneration. The terms and conditions of the use of the licensed property are defined in the body of a license agreement which constitutes the "formal permission."

The licensed property which is the subject of the agreement may be one or a number of patents, or even pending patent applications. The licensed property can include both domestic and foreign patents and applications or simply foreign applications. Similarly, technology and know-how may also form part of the licensed property. It is not uncommon for someone to take a license solely to use another's technology and know-how.

The licensed property may also include other forms of intellectual property, for example copyrights and trade secrets, which are commonly used to protect computer software and its source and object codes. In addition, trademark and service mark rights may be bundled with the package of property rights. This is frequently the case where a foreign licensee seeks to take all rights to manufacture and market a domestic product for international sales and distribution.

While there are a multitude of different ways to compensate a licensor for the use of its intellectual property rights, the royalty is far and away the most common. A "royalty" is a percentage of the licensee's sales of products which incorporate the intellectual property rights. Advances and guaranteed minimum royalties are not uncommon in technology licensing. In certain instances, licensing fees may be charged as well.

For the license to work, the licensed property must be protectable under the intellectual property laws or otherwise unavailable to the licensee. By taking a license, the licensee is agreeing to pay the licensor for the right to do something it could not otherwise do. It is the license grant that gives the licensee the right or permission to use the property and the reason the licensee is willing to pay some form of consideration for the right. If the underlying licensed property is in the public domain and free for adoption and use by anyone, there would be no reason for anyone to consider entering into a license agreement and paying a royalty for such right.

Licensing Benefits: The Licensor's Perspective

Why would a property owner want to permit others to use its intellectual property rights? Why would anyone want to put a potential competitor in business? Licensing is big business, and there are many reasons for companies to grant licenses for the use of their technology. Perhaps the most common is the allure of adding bottom line profit with little effort and risk on the part of the licensor. Many companies view licensing as a vehicle to become the next IBM or Texas Instruments. Based on the success of many licensing programs, it is difficult to challenge that notion.

Some licensors view licensing as a risk-free (and profitable) way of entering a market without having to make a heavy investment in capital equipment and personnel. In this way, the licensor avoids many of the risks associated with developing a new product line. In actual fact, the risk of the venture actually passes to the licensee. The licensor may even include guaranteed minimum royalties in the license agreement, where the licensee would have to pay the licensor even in the face of total failure.

Similarly, many licensors look upon licensing as a way to penetrate markets that they had, heretofore, been unable or unwilling to enter. For example, a domestic company may have a lock on a particular market in the United States but have little ability to penetrate foreign markets. Licensing manufacturers around the world is an effective way to develop international sales using licensees who work regularly in these markets or who have the necessary expertise. Moreover, such a program is totally complementary to the licensor's efforts in the original country of manufacture, and the synergy formed by such a relationship can be mutually beneficial.

Concrete examples of how licensing technology can increase market share and strength are found in the approaches taken by IBM and Apple Computer with respect to their operating systems. Early on, IBM treated its PC system as an "open box" and readily granted licenses to third parties to use the system and develop their own products under license from IBM. The risk they ran, of course, was that the licensees would eventually become IBM's stiffest competitors. The competition did appear and many licensees prospered by taking a license from IBM. Conversely, Apple Computer treated its operating system as a "closed box" and actively discouraged others from using the system or building clones. As a result, there are virtually no Macintosh clones on the market today.

Which was the more effective approach? After a decade of sales, IBM stock was selling at or close to an all-time high, while Apple Computer was having difficulty surviving. The IBM PC system became the industry standard while the Macintosh system (which many believe to be technically superior and infinitely easier to use) was relegated to specialty and niche markets. While it would be overly simplistic to attribute IBM's success and Apple's problems to the licensing approaches set out over a decade ago, there can be little argument that IBM's licensing strategy was largely responsible for the widespread acceptance of the PC in the marketplace, albeit through the efforts of many of IBM's own competitors and licensees. In stark contrast, Apple's Macintosh sales lagged far behind. This tends to validate the old theory that a small piece of an enormous pie is better than all of a small one.

Licensing Benefits: The Licensee's Perspective

Why would a manufacturer consider entering into a license agreement and pay a royalty instead of developing its own proprietary property which could be used free and clear (and even potentially licensed to others)? A licensee's reasons for entering into a license agreement also vary widely. In many instances, the licensee simply does not have a choice. Where the licensor has a dominant patent or patents which cover a particular product line, the licensee is faced with the choice of either abandoning the thought of producing such a product until expiration of the patent or challenging the patent in court. The risks involved with challenging a patent are substantial, and many licensees would simply rather pay a royalty to the property owner than pay legal fees to a law firm who will initiate and conduct a law suit where there are no guarantees.

Other licensees look upon licensing more positively. They believe that the right license will permit them to enter a market that they had been unable to penetrate before. These licensees view the royalty as a small price to pay for the jump start that the license gives them. Faced with the prospect of spending millions and even billions of dollars in research and product development versus paying a percentage of its sales to a licensor who has already made that investment, many licensees quickly ask "Where do I sign?" Some view it as "renting" versus "buying."

While the motivations for each party coming to the negotiating table may differ, one thing is constant: licensing works. A good license benefits both parties, and that is the reason licensing remains so popular.

Licensing In vs. Licensing Out

A company can essentially engage in two types of licensing: "licensing in" and "licensing out." As the terms imply, "licensing in" occurs when a company takes in a new license from another party. In this situation, the company becomes the licensee. "Licensing out" occurs when a company which owns or controls an intellectual property right grants licenses to other parties to use the rights.

There are, of course, hybrid versions of the two. It is not uncommon for two companies, each of which owns intellectual property, to enter into a "cross licensing" relationship. This means very simply that each will permit the other to use its intellectual property subject to certain conditions defined in the license agreement. While such cross licensing agreements can be royalty bearing, they don't have to be, since each party receives an advantage in exchange for permitting the other to use its intellectual property rights. Obviously, there has to be some balance between the respective contributions of each party.

As one can readily appreciate, the mind set and problems facing a company "licensing in" are different than "licensing out." Nevertheless, the issues are the same and are frequently resolved in the same way.

What Are the Risks?

Every thing worth doing has some attendant risk. Entering into a license agreement is no exception. The licensor who simply sits back and waits for the revenues to pour in is a fool. Similarly, the licensee who thinks that a license will solve all of its problems is naive. Successful businessmen are neither foolhardy nor naive. While licensing presents far fewer risks than attempting to build a new business, the path is not devoid of all risk. Many of the potential hazards can, however, be addressed and resolved to everyone's satisfaction in the license agreement. That is what both parties should strive for.

What are the licensor's risks? Apart from the obvious risk of not getting paid for the use of its intellectual property rights, the licensor actually faces much greater problems. For example, by permitting another to use its intellectual property rights, the licensor is potentially putting these rights in jeopardy. The failure of the licensee to properly mark products can limit the licensor's ability to pursue and collect from infringers. Where the licensed property includes trademark rights, the licensor's failure to exercise quality control over the ultimate licensed products can be considered "naked licensing" which can result in the loss of underlying trademark rights.

A potentially more serious risk affecting a licensor involves product liability exposure. Should the licensed products cause injury or death to a third party, there is the possibility that the licensor can be brought into the action as a target defendant. Where the licensed property includes trademarks, this becomes a very real possibility.

As part of any license agreement, a licensor will be asked to make certain representations and warranties relative to the licensed property. The licensor will typically be asked to warrant that the licensee's use of the licensed property and its sale of licensed products will not infringe upon the rights of any third party. Moreover, most license agreements will include a companion indemnification provision which states that in the event the licensee becomes the subject of an infringement action by a third party based on its use of such licensed property, the licensor shall defend and indemnify the licensee.

Simply stated, that means that if the licensee gets sued for infringement, the licensor is potentially liable for both the cost of the defense and any potential recovery. In today's litigious society, a lawsuit is a very real possibility.

The risks facing a licensee in a licensing program are fewer in number than those of the licensor, but potentially greater in magnitude. The greatest liability of the licensee involves its contractual obligations to the licensor under the license agreement. These obligations may include advances and guaranteed minimum royalty payments. Thus, a licensee faces the potentially unpalatable prospect of having to pay the licensor a guaranteed minimum royalty for products that never make it to market.

Two:
Getting Started

You are now ready to take the plunge into licensing. What does that mean and how do you go about getting started? Your initial steps will largely depend on which side of the licensing table you eventually land. Will you be the property owner/licensor who will be "licensing out" or the manufacturer/licensee who will be "licensing in" another's patents and technology?

Licensing Out

With few exceptions, a licensor must be a property owner. Simply stated, that means that the licensor must be the owner of certain intellectual property rights (e.g., patents, trademarks, copyrights, technology). Ownership of such rights is an essential element of a licensing transaction since few will agree to pay for something that the licensor does not own. The licensor will be expected to warrant to a licensee that it is the owner of the underlying intellectual property rights. Should someone else subsequently make a claim of ownership to such rights, the licensor will normally be required to defend and indemnify the licensee against such claim.

This does not mean that the patents or technology have to be developed in-house. There are many instances where a company acquires intellectual property rights from one party by assignment and then turns around and licenses those rights to another party.

There are also situations where "beneficial owners" of intellectual property rights are able to license rights to a third party. For example, an exclusive licensee with the right to grant sublicenses would be able to "sublicense" these rights to another, subject to any restrictions imposed on the exclusive licensee in the underlying license agreement with the licensor.

Sources of Licensable Technology

Where do licensing properties come from? With companies such as IBM or General Electric, the answer is easy. The starting point for licensing out would be the thousands of patents in their patent portfolio. With smaller entities, however, the search may become a bit more difficult. One would begin, of course, with the company's portfolio of issued patents and pending patent applications. Close attention should be paid to the foreign patents and pending applications.

Potential licensors should not overlook copyright rights, particularly those covering operating software. As will be explained later, copyright rights are effective upon creation, not registration with the Copyright Office. As such, the search for licensable properties should not be restricted to registrations with the Copyright Office. Another point to remember is that copyright rights are international in scope. Thus, valid United States copyright registrations can form the basis of a licensing program in Brazil, for example.

The trademark portfolio should also be reviewed to determine what trademark rights the potential licensor owns. Again, particular attention should be paid to the international registrations and applications therefore.

Licensees will pay for the right to use a company's technology and know-how as well its trade secrets. Unfortunately, identifying potentially licensable technology and know-how can oftentimes be difficult since these rights can be somewhat amorphous by nature.

The starting and ending points for a licensable property search is a series of discussions with the company's chief engineer (or head of research and development) and patent counsel. These individuals will, no doubt, have the best feel for the company's potentially licensable properties since they are working in that area daily. Don't forget to discuss the issue with the company's sales or marketing executives. The company's Vice-President of Marketing should have a good understanding of the marketplace and can frequently provide some valuable insight into what the competition might be seeking.

The inquiry should not be limited solely to those patents and technology used by the company in its day-to-day business operations. While concededly they have the greatest value to the company, there may be some reluctance to license them to others, particularly competitors. Therefore, the licensing administrator should look very closely at those patents and technology which are either underutilized or not utilized at all. Licensing out these patents or technology to non-competitors in ancillary fields can be a boon to the licensor, since there is potential to generate income without impacting the company's core business. The same is true of international patent rights which are not currently being utilized (or are underutilized) by the company.

Setting Up the Framework

While many executives think that licensing is easy, those that work in the field know otherwise. To some it may look easy because a good licensing administrator has spent the time to properly organize the department and supervise the process. Upon making the decision to embark on a "licensing out" program, the first order of business for the potential licensor is to implement a licensing plan. The licensing plan should list the tasks that need to be performed in order to develop a solid licensing program and identify the individual or individuals who will have the responsibility to perform such tasks. The more the potential licensor is organized going in, the easier the program will be to implement and run.

In order to identify the tasks, the administrator might want to consult with the company's legal and patent departments, engineering and R&D professionals and marketing personnel. Seeking their input and advice at this early stage will facilitate the entire process. Don't overlook the fact that there will be substantial administrative and computer support help needed. Plan accordingly.

Last, but not least, a preliminary budget for the entire process should be established, and a project schedule should be developed. Both short-term and long-term goals should be established at the outset, and the department's performance relative to these goals should be regularly reviewed. Despite the best laid plans of mice and men, the licensor might discover down the road that the market is simply not willing to pay for the right to use its intellectual property. The objective should not be to create a black hole. If the market does not respond, there are alternatives to running the department at a loss. For example, the program could be turned over to an outside commissioned agent or broker or even shut down.

Creating a Marketing Plan

Some view licensing as a marketing function. This is quite true. Few intellectual property owners can simply sit back and wait for the telephone to ring with offers from prospective licensees. Most good licensors spend a considerable amount of time, effort and money in marketing their licenses and their properties.

For this reason, licensors should view licensing in the same vein as marketing. Companies regularly require that their marketing executives develop a marketing plan prior to the introduction of a new product. The same should be true for licensing. Before embarking on a licensing program, the responsible licensing executive should develop a marketing plan for the program. The plan should include:

- an identification of potentially licensable properties;
- the status of legal protection for the licensable properties;
- an analysis of the competition;
- a list of potential licensees;
- a schedule for the implementation of the licensing program; and
- a budget for the licensing program.

Licensing is a business and should be structured and run accordingly.

The Role of a Consultant or Agent

There are two principal ways to conduct a licensing program. The first is to create a licensing department which will go out and seek potential licensees and administer the program. The second is to turn the entire program over to an outside licensing agent who will assume full responsibility for the program.

When a company creates its own internal licensing department, all of the income derived from licensing remains with the company. There is, obviously, a large risk to this approach since it assumes that the program will be successful or, at least, self-sufficient. If the program fails, all costs associated with the development program are lost. The costs associated with the creation of a licensing program can be quite high, particularly if experienced, high-priced licensing professionals are brought on board or retained as consultants.

The alternative approach is to turn the entire program over to an outside agent or broker who will develop and administer the program. Licensing agents are frequently used in other areas of licensing, merchandising most notably. They are, however, less frequently employed in the patent and technology area.

Most licensing agents will work for a percentage of the income that they generate for the licensor. The usual percentage ranges from ten to fifty percent of the gross income derived from the licensing program. The actual percentage will depend in large measure on the strength of the properties involved. In addition, most agents will seek an ongoing retainer fee which may (or may not) be applied as an advance against their commission.

The "consultant" is more commonly used in patent and technology licensing. Frequently, the consultant is an experienced licensing executive who previously worked for a major licensor. Consultants bring with them decades of experience in the licensing community and can quickly assist a new company in developing a licensing program. Typically, consultants work on an hourly or per diem basis, although some will work on a flat fee or even a percentage basis. The retention of a consultant for the new licensor can pay tremendous dividends down the road.

A list of such consultants is found in the appendix to this work. The Licensing Executive Society ("LES") also periodically publishes an updated list of technology consultants.

The Lawyer is Your Friend

If you really want to develop a good licensing program, you must put on some old clothes, turn down the lights, light a candle and recite the following incantation at least twice, "The lawyer is my friend."

Like it or not, lawyers play an integral role in patent and technology licensing. The intellectual property rights being licensed are protected under the intellectual property laws, typically attributable to the efforts of the company's patent counsel. After the licensing executive identifies an appropriate licensee, the licensing relationship will be formed by the preparation and execution of a license agreement. That agreement will, no doubt, be prepared and negotiated by the company's patent or licensing counsel. At virtually every step of the process, the licensing executive will be joined at the hip with the company's lawyers.

Lawyers frequently have the reputation as being deal killers. Concededly, some are. The vast majority, however, are not. The licensing professional must appreciate that the role of the lawyer is to protect its clients. Unfortunately, some do not know where to draw the line.

It has always been our experience that where there is a good working relationship between the licensing executive and the licensing lawyer, the deal runs smoothly. Deals break down when the relationship breaks down. Where there is an open line of communication and a clear delineation of responsibility, however, the process almost always works well. Keep those lines of communication open and you will be amazed at what can be accomplished.

Finding the Right Licensees

You've prepared the potential "victims" list and are now ready to go out and begin marketing the licenses. Who do you go to first?

While the obvious inclination may be to start with the Fortune 50 list and work backward, size or sales volume should not be the governing factor in selecting the "right" licensee. While the eventual license agreement will state that the licensor and licensee are not partners in a legal sense, in a business sense they are.

Licensors should seek licensees that they feel comfortable working with. The licensee will be using the licensor's intellectual property rights and has the potential to expose it to some degree of risk. As such, simple sales revenue should not be the sole criteria in selecting a licensee. There must be a certain "fit" for both parties.

The licensor should pay particular attention to the ability of the licensee to produce quality products. The licensor should not rely on verbal assurances of quality by the licensee. The licensor should fully investigate the history of the licensee. No matter how onerous the eventual license agreement may be, leopards do not change their spots. A licensee who has always produced low quality products will not find salvation simply because of the existence of a license agreement that requires it.

Licensing In

A licensee who is taking a license to use another's patent or technology has different concerns than the licensor/property owner. While many licensors have created expansive licensing departments, that is not normally the case with licensees. A large number of licensees are "one shot" licensees. That is, they identify a particular patent or area of technology where they need assistance, obtain a license to use that patent or technology and go their merry way, never again to enter the licensing arena.

The obligations and responsibilities of a licensee are typically far fewer than those of a licensor. The licensee is normally unconcerned about the issues of protection and enforcement of intellectual property rights. The burden of seeking and maintaining patent and trademark protection falls on the licensor's shoulders. If there is any third party infringement, that is also the licensor's responsibility.

Licensees must report their sales and pay royalties. For many that is their one and only responsibility. Depending upon the property involved, some licensees will be required to periodically submit product for approval by the licensor, perhaps once or twice a year. The licensee's principal responsibility is to use the patents and/or technology to manufacture and sell products. That is what they do for a living.

With such minimal responsibilities, most licensees do not go to the trouble of establishing elaborate or sophisticated licensing departments. There is simply no need for them. What they need, however, is a good royalty accounting system and a docketing system for telling them when products need to be submitted to the licensor for review and approval.

Identifying a Need

What types of needs motivate a licensee to enter into a license agreement? A relatively large number of license agreements are negotiated after a property owner has notified the manufacturer that it is infringing its intellectual property rights. Rather than agreeing to cease and desist from selling these products in the future, the manufacturer agrees to negotiate a license agreement with the property owner which permits the licensee to continue to sell such products while compensating the licensor in the form of a royalty based on such sales.

There are also some situations where licensees *must* take a license if they want to become a player in a particular industry. In the computer and audio industries, there are certain industry standard technologies which must be licensed. The Dolby noise reduction system is an example, If the licensee wants to sell a product that is "state of the art" and includes the features that all of its competitors include, it must license such technology and patents. Thus, it has a practical "need" to take such a license.

Alternatively, some licensees choose to take a license as an alternative to investing in product development. They decide to go into a particular product area or create a particular product line. In the course of researching the area as a prelude to the commencement of a product development program, they come across a patent or patents of another which are controlling. Rather than attempt to design around these patents, they choose to work out a licensing arrangement with their owner for the use of the patents and any associated technology. In such instance, the "need" is to avoid the expenditure of large sums of money associated with new product development.

Other licensees are actually nominal competitors of a property owner, frequently in a different territory. For example, a United States manufacturer might look to technology developed by a French company which markets similar products on the continent. Believing that there is a market for such product in this country, the United States company may approach the French company to license its technology and know-how as well as any United States patents they might have. The "need" is a substitution for new product development.

Locating Compatible Technology or Patents

How does one find compatible technology or patents? If the licensee has been put on notice that it is infringing another's intellectual property rights, the search stops with the cease and desist letter. It is more common, however, for the licensee to voluntarily embark on a search for a particular property. Seeking out and finding potentially licensable patents and technology is infinitely easier today than it was decades ago. The "information superhighway" permits potential licensees to go "on-line" to instantly find all patents which relate to a particular field in virtually all countries. Copies of these patents can be downloaded in a matter of minutes and the manual review can begin.

Some of the major property owners/licensors have their own home pages on the World Wide Web describing what patents are available for licensing. A web crawler search can quickly turn up some potentially licensable properties.

Marketing and technical executives who regularly work in a particular field have a general understanding and knowledge of what technology is available and potentially licensable. Consultation with these individuals can be invaluable.

Last, but not least, there are consultants and brokers who are in the business of bringing licenses to licensees. Contacting such individuals can prove helpful when attempting to find licensable technology, particularly if the consultant happens to be representing the property owner.

Approaching the Property Owner

Don't be shy! If you are thinking of licensing another's patents or technology, call up the licensing executive (if there is one) and see whether there may be some common interest in entering into a mutually beneficial license agreement. If you're unsure about who to call, check with the Licensing Executive Society ("LES") to see whether the property owner is a member and, if so, who is the responsible individual at the company.

If you strike out going through LES, try going through the in-house patent counsel or the general counsel. They will frequently be able to put you in touch with the relevant individual if they don't have that responsibility themselves. If there are no in-house lawyers, try the head of research and development or the chief engineer.

If none of these positions exist and you still believe there is something there, call the president of the company. He or she would certainly know whether there is any interest in entering into such a license agreement.

THREE:
The Basics of Intellectual Property Law

This book would not be complete without an overview of the basics of intellectual property law. For those unfamiliar with the expression, the term "intellectual property" is frequently used to describe that which is protected by patents, trademarks and copyrights. The United States Constitution specifically provides for patent and copyright protection while trademark rights are based on the interstate commerce clause of the Constitution.

Intellectual property law will also frequently include unfair competition and trade secret law, as well as the rights of publicity and privacy. By and large, the legal community differentiates multimedia law, computer law and entertainment law from intellectual property law, although there are many common elements to each area.

Intellectual Property Law "101"

There is a great deal of confusion as to the differences between patent, trademark and copyright protection. Intellectual property attorneys are frequently asked by new clients to "patent" a new product name. Anyone familiar with intellectual property law knows

23

that one patents an invention, while a name is protected under the trademark laws.[1]

The problem (or luxury) facing the intellectual property attorney is that oftentimes a product or concept can be protected under a variety of different legal theories. For example, a three-dimensional object (for example, a new rolling machine) can be protected by a utility patent (covering the unique structure and interaction of the elements), a design patent (covering the aesthetic appearance of the machine) and a trademark registration (covering the name used to sell the machine). Moreover, if the machine incorporates a microprocessor, the software used to control the microprocessor may be protected under the copyright laws. Last, but not least, there may be a secret way in which the machine is manufactured or assembled which is known only to the employees. That unique manufacturing or assembly method may qualify as a trade secret. Thus, the same item can be protected under a

---

[1] See generally Borchard, A Trademark Is Not a Patent or a Copyright, United States Trademark Association (1990); and McCarthy, TRADEMARKS AND UNFAIR COMPETITION, §6.1-6.9. A number of excellent treatises have been written on the subjects of patent, trademark and copyright law and this text will not attempt to duplicate their generally thorough treatment of those subjects. Reference should be made, for example, to McCarthy, TRADEMARKS AND UNFAIR COMPETITION and Gilson, TRADEMARK PROTECTION AND PRACTICE with respect to trademark law; Deller, WALKER ON PATENTS and Rosenberg, PATENT LAW FUNDAMENTALS with respect to patent law; and NIMMER ON COPYRIGHT and Latman, THE COPYRIGHT LAW with respect to copyright law. This text will, instead, attempt to present a general overview of the subject of intellectual property law with particular emphasis on how the various forms of protection can be effectively used to protect merchandising properties.

variety of different legal theories, all of which can complement each other.

With the exception of copyright protection, all other forms of intellectual property protection are territorial in nature. That means that a United States patent or trademark registration will only protect that property right in the United States. Separate patents or trademark registrations must be obtained on a country-by-country basis to protect the product abroad. While the process of obtaining worldwide rights has been simplified over the years as a result of the United States becoming a member of a number of different international conventions, obtaining worldwide patent or trademark protection remains a lengthy and expensive proposition.

Obtaining worldwide copyright rights is, however, substantially easier and infinitely less expensive. Due to a number of international conventions to which the United States is a signatory party, copyright protection is international in scope. Thus, a valid United States copyright registration will protect the creator from infringement in virtually every other country in the world.

Trade secret protection is available in the United States, provided that certain positive steps are taken by the property owner to preserve the secret. While many countries outside the United States recognize the concept, its application varies from country to country. Thus, before relying on trade secret protection in a particular country, it is a good idea to consult with a local intellectual property attorney in that country.

Patents

There are three principal forms of patents: utility patents, design patents and plant patents. (See 35 U.S.C. § 1 et seq.) In the United States, utility patents are granted by the United States Patent and Trademark Office (the "PTO") and are good for a single term of either seventeen years from the registration date or twenty years from the filing date (depending upon when the application was filed). Design patents are good for a fourteen-year term from the date of issuance. Plant patents are good for the same term as utility patents. All patent terms are non-renewable.

Utility patents cover any new and useful process, machine, manufacture, or composition of matter or any new and useful improvements thereon. The term "process" is defined by the Patent Act, (35 U.S.C. § 100), as a "process, art or method, and includes a new use of a known process, machine, manufacture, composition of matter, or material." Generally speaking, one may obtain a patent for such a process, machine, manufacture or composition of matter *unless* it: (1) was known or used by others in the United States or patented or described in a printed publication in any country before the invention by the applicant (35 U.S.C. § 102(a)) or, (2) if different than such prior invention, such differences would have been obvious to one skilled in the art (35 U.S.C. § 103).

Design patents cover any new, original and ornamental design for an article of manufacture. The patentability of designs is subject to the same standards as utility patents. Plant patents protect anyone who invents, discovers or asexually reproduces any distinct and new variety of plant, including cultivated spores, mutants, hybrids and newly found seedlings, other than a tuber propagated plant or a plant found in an uncultivated state. The patentability of plants is subject to the same standards as utility and design patents.

No Protection During the Patent Pending Stage

Patent protection is only effective upon the issuance of a patent and then only in the country in which the patent has issued. Accordingly, no protection is granted during the "patent pending" period. Similarly, a United States patent will not prevent a company in England from manufacturing and selling an otherwise infringing product outside the United States.

The grant of a U.S. patent confers upon the inventor the exclusive right to make, use and sell his or her invention throughout the United States during the term of the patent. As this is an exclusive grant, any other person who makes, uses or sells any patent invention within the United States during the term of the patent is an infringer of the patent as is anyone who actively induces infringement of the patent. The grant of a patent gives the inventor not only the right to exclude those who may have actually copied the patented invention but also those who, with no knowledge whatsoever of the patent, may have independently created the same invention after the inventor had conceived his or her invention.

The Patent Process

The process of obtaining a patent is, in theory, relatively simple. The inventor's patent attorney prepares and files a patent application with the U.S. Patent and Trademark Office together with a filing fee, which is generally between $500 and $1,000 (depending upon the size of the entity owning the invention and the number of claims). The applicant must swear in a declaration or affidavit that he is the original and first inventor of the invention and must disclose all relevant material to the PTO.

A PTO examiner then reviews the application for form and conducts a search to determine whether the invention is novel. The examiner will then issue an Office Action that either allows or rejects the application. If the examiner rejects the application, he will give the reasons for the rejection and list any prior patents found by the examiner in the course of the search.

The applicant may respond to this Office Action by filing an amendment or response. This begins the patent prosecution phase, and there can be a number of back and forths between the PTO and the applicant until such time as the application is either allowed or finally rejected. Failure to respond within the statutory time period (typically up to a maximum of six months) will result in abandonment of the application. The PTO has implemented a Shortened Statutory Period for response (typically three months). While the applicant can respond beyond this Shortened Statutory Period, such a response is subject to the payment of a fee.

Assuming that the application is allowed, the PTO requires the payment of an issue fee and, upon payment of that fee, a formal patent will be issued. While a relatively high percentage of patent applications are allowed each year, there are many that are rejected. Upon the issuance of a final rejection by the PTO examiner, the applicant has a number of choices: (1) amend the application to place it in condition for allowance without raising new issues; (2) abandon the application; (3) appeal the final rejection to the PTO Board of Appeals; or (4) refile the application as either a continuation application or a continuation in part application to continue prosecution.

The inventor should anticipate that the entire process, from start to finish and assuming a favorable outcome, will take between one and three years and cost between $3,000 and $10,000, depending upon the complexity of the invention and the difficulty experienced in prosecution. The cost for filing a relatively simple utility patent with the PTO (without considering additional costs and fees for prosecution and issuance) is typically at least $2,500, including attorney's fees, filing costs and draftsman charges. Design patent applications typically cost at least $900 in attorney's fees, PTO fees and drawings.

Once a patent issues, the patent owner will be required to pay taxes or maintenance fees on the patent at three intervals during the patent's lifetime. Failure to pay these maintenance fees will result in cancellation of the patent. The actual amount of these maintenance fees changes almost annually and are always regressive. Thus, the maintenance fee for the first maintenance period will be substantially lower than the fee for the second maintenance period which, in turn, will be substantially lower than the fee for the third period. The PTO's philosophy is to encourage owners of patents that are not being used to permit them to go abandoned.

Trademarks

Trademark protection is available for letters, words, names, abbreviations, acronyms, monograms, phrases, slogans, titles, symbols, numerals, logos, devices, character or personality images, pictures, labels, shapes, packages, configurations of goods, or combinations thereof. (See 15 U.S.C. § 1501 et seq.) The Supreme Court has recently added colors to the list of potential trademarks. The criterion for protectability under the trademark laws is that the mark must be distinctive, that is, it must be capable of distinguishing the owner's products or services from those of another in interstate commerce. Simply stated, the mark must serve as an indicator of source, origin or sponsorship.

We all know the COCA-COLA trademark, which serves to identify a particular brand of soft drink from the competition. Trademark protection has also now extended to such diverse forms of indicators as product shapes (the MOGEN DAVID wine bottle), colors (pink for fiberglass insulation), character images ("SNOOPY on a doghouse") and logos (the NIKE "swoosh" stripe). The applicant must demonstrate that the mark is or has become distinctive and, as such, serves as an indicator of source, origin or sponsorship. Frequently, the PTO and/or the courts will look to long years of exclusive use and extensive advertising or promotion to infer distinctiveness.

In the patent and technology licensing areas, trademarks typically play a secondary role. The licensor of a patented process or product may occasionally grant the licensee the right to use the trademark under which the process or product is sold. In such instance, the trademark license grant may be incorporated into the patent license agreement. Alternatively, it could take the form of a separate agreement depending upon the wishes of the parties.

Trademark rights in the United States are based

on use, not registration. That differs from other countries where trademark rights are based almost exclusively on registration. In the United States, the first to use a mark in interstate commerce on a particular product or service will typically have superior rights to second comers.

Since trademark rights are use-based, the product or service on which the mark is used is highly relevant. Trademarks are classified into 42 different classes depending upon the product or service. One may obtain rights in a particular mark in one class while another has rights for that same mark in another class. Consider, for example, PARAMOUNT chicken and PARAMOUNT PICTURES. These are both registered trademarks. The test applied by courts and the Patent and Trademark Office is whether there would be any likelihood of confusion between the two uses.

While trademark rights are created upon the commencement of use, it is always wise to register the mark with the PTO where there is use in interstate commerce. A trademark owner can also obtain appropriate state trademark registrations for marks that are used on an intrastate basis. Registration of a mark serves as notice to the public that you consider yourself to be the owner of the mark and also serves as a deterrent to adoption and use by others. Moreover, a registration offers numerous procedural advantages in litigation when attempting to sue infringers.

An application to register a mark with the PTO can be filed based on either actual use of the mark in commerce or on a bona fide intention to use the mark in commerce. No registration will issue unless actual use is effected, however. The current PTO fee for filing a trademark application is $245 per class. The cost of filing and prosecuting a trademark application through an attorney with normal prosecution will typically be about $1000 for a single class application. From start to finish, an applicant should expect that it will take at least a year before any registration issues. Unlike the case with patent protection, however, the owner of an unregistered trademark can bring an action against an infringer under state common law or under the false designation of origin section of the Lanham Act.

Federal trademark registrations have terms of ten years. Use must be demonstrated during the fifth and sixth year of the initial term in order to maintain the registration. Trademark registrations may be renewed indefinitely for additional ten-year terms provided that use of the trademark continues. As a result, a trademark registration can be granted for as long as the mark is in use, provided that the proper maintenance fees and procedures are followed. Trademark registrations for marks that are not being used are subject to attack and cancellation.

Copyrights

Copyright protection finds its genesis in the United States Constitution and covers any works of authorship fixed in a tangible medium of expression, now known or later developed, from which they can be perceived, reproduced or otherwise communicated, either directly or with the aid of a machine. See 17 U.S.C. § 101 et seq.

Works of authorship for copyright purposes include the following categories:

1. literary works;

2. musical works, including any accompanying words;
3. dramatic works, including any accompanying music;
4. pantomimes and choreographic works;
5. pictorial, graphic and sculptural works;
6. motion pictures and other audiovisual works;
7. sound recordings; and
8. architectural works.

While manufacturers have used the copyright laws for years to protect their catalogs, sell sheets, instructional manuals and other printed matter, copyright protection has now become the principal way in which to protect computer software. Both the source and object codes for computer software are subject to copyright protection.

Virtually all software is entitled to copyright protection, provided that it is "original." The owner of a copyrighted work, according to the Copyright Act, has the right:

1. to reproduce the copyrighted works in copies or phonorecords;
2. to prepare derivative works based upon the copyrighted work;
3. to distribute copies or phonorecords of the copyrighted work to the public by sale or other transfer of ownership, or by rental, lease, or lending;
4. in the case of literary, musical, dramatic, and choreographic works, pantomimes, and motion pictures and other audiovisual works, to perform the copyrighted work publicly; and
5. in the case of literary, musical, dramatic and choreographic works, pantomimes, and picto-

rial, graphic, or sculptural works, including the individual images of a motion picture or other audio visual work, to display the copyrighted work publicly.

Copyright rights begin at the moment of the creation of the work — not when the Copyright Office registers the copyright. However, registration of a copyright claim with the Copyright Office is a prerequisite to commencing an infringement action. A delay in registering a copyright with the Copyright Office may prevent the copyright owner from seeking statutory damages and recovering its attorney's fees in a litigation. As such, it is wise for authors to register their copyrights during the early stages of creation.

Registering a copyright with the United States Copyright Office is very simple. The Copyright Office provides the form which must be completed for registration. For computer software, Form TX is used. For most printed matter, Form TX is used, while artwork is protected using Form VA. The Copyright Office instructions accompanying each type of copyright application are excellent. Samples of such copyright applications are contained in the Appendices to this work. The current filing fee for a copyright application is $20. It currently takes between three and four months for the Copyright Office to act on and register claims. This time period can be accelerated to a matter of weeks by paying a surcharge to expedite the application. The current fee for an expedited application is $400. Usually, the services of an attorney are not required. Many authors, artists and programmers regularly fill and file their own copyright applications.

Copyright rights vest with the creator of the copyrightable material unless the creator is an employee of a company and performed such work as part of his or her position or, alternatively, where the creator was specifically retained as a contractor to create such work. In the latter case, the contractor agreement must specifically recite that any work performed under the agreement is to be deemed a work made for hire and is thus owned by the company. Failure to address this issue may result in the creator retaining the copyright rights in the work even though he or she may have been paid to perform such work.

For works created after January 1, 1978, the term of copyright protection is the life of the author plus fifty years. Works made for hire have a term of seventy-five years from the year of first publication or 100 years from the date of creation, whichever expires first.

Unfair Competition

The laws of unfair competition are founded on the premise that one may not sell its goods in such a way as to make it appear that they come from another source. By and large, unfair competition finds its basis in state common law, although Section 43(a) of the Lanham Act, which prohibits false designation of origin, has been referred to as the federal unfair competition statute.

Many states have recently adopted unfair trade practices acts. The advantage of many of these acts is that they provide for the recoupment of attorneys' fees for the prevailing party as well as the trebling of damages under appropriate circumstances.

Other Forms of Intellectual Property Protection

Other forms of protection available to protect licensing properties include state trademark registrations and federal and state anti-dilution statutes. There are times when there are distinct advantages in obtaining state trademark registrations, for example, in those jurisdictions that tie remedies against counterfeiting to state registrations. Additionally, there are times when state anti-dilution protection should be considered, particularly where the problem does not involve goods that are in direct competition with those of the property owner or his licensees, but rather, involves use of the property or a confusingly similar property on unrelated goods of someone unrelated to the property owner. Such unrelated use will dilute, if not destroy, the value of the mark in this regard. A number of states have passed such anti-dilution statutes, and at the writing of this book, the President had recently signed into law a bill (H.R. 1295) which would amend the Lanham Act to protect certain famous trademarks from dilution.

Common law forms of protection available for protecting licensing and merchandising properties include common law trademark protection, unfair competition, the palming off of goods and the right of publicity. Whenever possible, however, these forms of protection should be viewed as an adjunct to — not a substitute for — statutory protection. There are a number of disadvantages in relying solely on common law protection over statutory protection. Property owners who opt only for common law protection may be held to a higher standard of proof than those who also obtain a federal trademark or copyright registration. In such instances, a property owner may be forced to establish that a particular property has acquired "secondary meaning" in the minds of the consuming public. Such proof is not required for statutory trademark protection.

Overlapping Forms of Protection

The fact that patents, trademarks and copyrights are separate and distinct forms of federal statutory protection does not preclude protection of a concept under several of these forms of protection. In many industries, these forms of protection are commonly combined to provide the strongest possible protection. The most common areas of overlap are between copyrights and trademarks, between design patents and trademarks and between copyrights and design patents.

It is not uncommon to obtain both trademark and copyright protection for the same artwork, with the copyright protecting its creative or artistic aspect and the trademark protecting it as an indicator of source, origin or sponsorship of the product on which the artwork is applied. By way of example, consider the artistic rendering of SNOOPY sitting on his doghouse basking in the noonday sun. Such an artistic rendering is generally protectable under the copyright laws. When that same rendering is incorporated into a decal and applied to the front of a T-shirt, it is protectable as a trademark since it serves as an indicator of source of that T-shirt by United Feature Syndicate, the owner of the licensing and merchandising rights to the SNOOPY property.

In *Frederick Warne & Co. v. Book Sales, Inc.*, 481 F. Supp. 1191, 1195-1196, 205 USPQ 444, 449 (S.D.N.Y. 1979), the court recognized the validity of dual protection under the trademark and copyright statutes, stating:

> Dual protection under copyright and trademark laws is particularly appropriate for graphic representations of characters. A character is deemed an artistic creation deserving copyright protection . . . [it] may also serve to identify the creator, thus meriting protection under theories of trademark or unfair competition . . . . Indeed, because of their special value in distinguishing goods and services, names and pictorial representations of characters are often registered as trademarks under the Lanham Act.

It is important to note the differences between copyright and trademark terms. Copyright protection is limited to a term of the life of the author plus 50 years for individuals; or a term of 75 years from the first publication (or 100 years from creation, whichever expires first) for works made for hire by employees. In contrast, the initial term for a registered trademark is ten years, and it may be renewed for like terms so long as the mark is being used. The *Frederick Warne* court viewed this difference in trademark and copyright statutes in the following manner:

> The fact that a copyrightable design has fallen into the public domain should not preclude protection under the trademark laws so long as it is shown to have acquired independent trademark significance, identifying in some way the source or sponsorship of the goods. See *Wyatt Earp Enterprises v. Sackman, Inc.*,

157 F. Supp. 621, 116 USPQ 122 (S.D.N.Y. 1958). Because the nature of the property right conferred by copyright is significantly different from that of trademark, trademark protection should be able to co-exist, and possibly overlap, with copyright protection without posing preemption difficulties.

Similarly, courts have repeatedly held that trademark and design patent protection can coexist. The leading case on the coexistence of design patents and trademarks is *In re Mogen David Wine Corp.*, 372 F.2d 539, 152 USPQ 593 (C.C.P.A. 1967). In that case, the Court of Customs and Patent Appeals recognized that the underlying purpose and essence of patent rights are separate and distinct from those pertaining to trademarks, and consequently the two forms of protection can coexist. Moreover, the court held that reliance on trademark protection after patent protection expires is permissible since, in the opinion of the court, such reliance beyond the expiration of a design patent does not extend the patent monopoly. The court recognized that the two forms of protection existed independently and that the termination of either had no legal effect on the continuance of the other. Courts have also recognized that there is a permissible overlap in the protection available through design patents and copyrights insofar as a design may qualify as a work of art.

Legal Notices

The use of appropriate legal notices is very important. Valuable property rights and the ability to collect damages may be lost as a result of the failure to comply with the requisite statutory notice provisions. The basic legal notices are the two trademark notices, the copyright notice, and the patent notice. ™ is used to designate a property that is considered a trademark by the owner, but one which is not federally registered. The ® symbol is used to designate a federally registered trademark — a trademark registered with the U.S. Patent and Trademark Office. The formal copyright notice requires the word "Copyright," the abbreviation "Copr.," or a © followed by the name of the copyright owner and the year of the work's first publication. Goods that are covered by a pending patent application should be marked "patent pending." Upon issuance of a patent, the "patent pending" notice should be replaced with a notice identifying the actual patent number, for example, "Patent No. 1,234,567."

Other notices that should be used include the legend "All Rights Reserved," which should follow the standard copyright notice. Use of this designation is particularly important when distribution is contemplated in South American countries. Many countries, including Canada, require products to bear a notice identifying the owner of the property and stating that the product is being manufactured by the licensee under license from the owner. The property owner should be aware of such requirements and make sure that all local laws are being complied with.

International Protection

As stated earlier, with the exception of copyright protection, most forms of intellectual property protection are territorial in nature. That means that if one seeks to cover a product or process outside the

United States, he or she must obtain appropriate intellectual property protection in each applicable country. While the filing for patent or trademark protection in foreign countries has been facilitated by several international conventions, it still remains a time-consuming and expensive proposition. For example, filing corresponding patent applications to a pending United States patent application may cost as much as $5,000 per country and frequently more in countries where translations are required.

The creation of the European Patent Office ("EPO") and the implementation of the Patent Cooperation Treaty have simplified the process and in certain instances, reduced the cost of the venture. Nevertheless, however, one should expect tremendous delay and extraordinary costs when seeking international patent protection.

Obtaining international trademark protection can also be time-consuming and costly. The adherence of the United States to the Madrid Protocol has begun to facilitate the process, although it is still wise to continue to file trademarks on a country-by-country basis.

The day of the international patent or trademark will come, although probably not in our lifetime. Until such time, patents and trademarks will remain largely territorial by nature.

FOUR:
Valuing Patents and Technology for Licensing*

Converting intellectual property into revenues, profits and value requires a framework of integrated complementary business assets. Complementary assets are needed to convert intellectual property into a product. These assets are needed to sell the product, distribute it, collect payments and implement the many business functions that are required for running a business. Companies that create intellectual property and then license it to others are still not free of the fundamental need for complementary assets. While licensors may not need to acquire and use complementary assets, successful commercialization of the licensed intellectual property is still dependent on organizing such assets. Royalty payments to the

---

*The authors would like to thank Russell L. Parr for preparing this chapter. Mr. Parr is President of Intellectual Property Research Associates, Yardley, Pennsylvania and Senior Vice President of AUS Consultants, Moorestown, New Jersey. His consulting assignments involve the value of patents, trademarks, copyrights and other intangible assets to help carry out strategic resource management, mergers, acquisitions, licensing transactions, transfer pricing and joint ventures. Mr. Parr also advises banks about the use of intangible assets as loan collateral and has served as an expert witness regarding intellectual property infringement damages. Mr. Parr is publisher of the highly respected **Licensin****nomics Review** which is dedicated to reporting d information about the economic aspects of intellectu erty licensing and joint venturing.

licensor are dependent upon the licensee organizing the needed complementary assets for exploitation of the licensed property.

Figure 1 shows the composition of a typical business enterprise. Basically, a business is comprised of working capital, fixed assets, intangible assets and intellectual property. Fixed assets include: manufacturing facilities, warehouses, office equipment, office furnishings, delivery vehicles, research equipment and other tangible equipment. This asset category is sometimes referred to as the "hard assets." The amount of funds invested in these categories can vary widely, according to the industry in which they participate. For example, huge investments in manufacturing assets are needed by companies in the automotive, aerospace, paper, semiconductor and telecommunications industries. In other industries, the manufacturing asset investment requirement is lower. Assemblers of electronic consumer goods arguably fall into this category. Also in this category are insurance brokers, computer software publishers, manufacturers of cosmetics and many business service companies.

Working capital is the net difference between the current assets and current liabilities.[1] Current assets are primarily composed of cash, accounts receivable and inventory. Current liabilities include accounts payable, accrued salary and other obligations due for payment. The net difference between current assets and current liabilities is the amount of working capital used in the business.

---

[1] Current assets are defined by generally-accepted accounting principles as assets which are expected to be converted into cash within twelve months of the date of the balance sheet on which they appear. Current liabilities are financial obligations that are expected to be satisfied within twelve months of the same date.

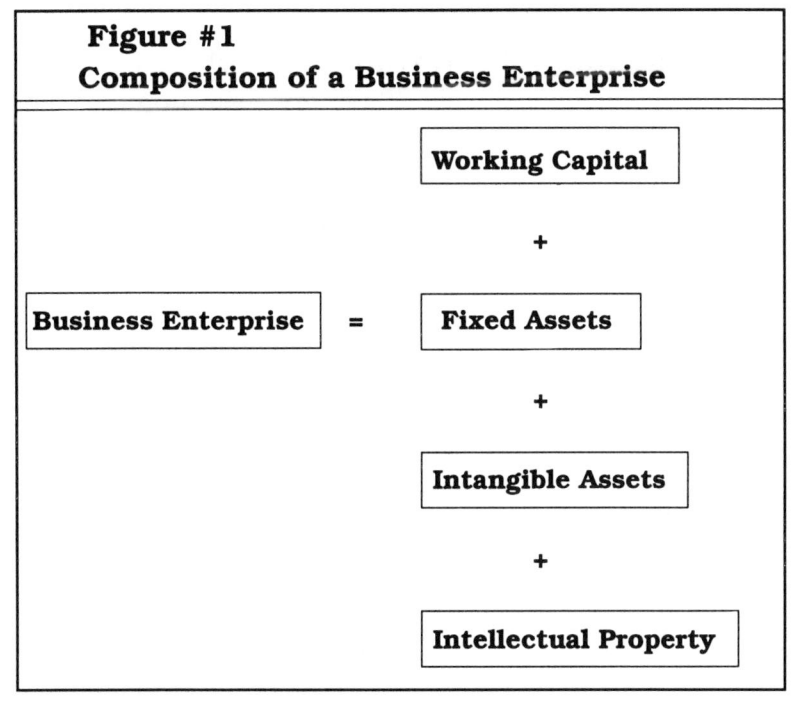

Figure #1
Composition of a Business Enterprise

Business Enterprise = Working Capital + Fixed Assets + Intangible Assets + Intellectual Property

    The investment requirements in working capital also varying by industry. The banking and insurance industries must maintain large amounts of working capital. By contrast, in the hotel industry, where raw materials and parts inventory are almost non-existent, working capital is a minor component of the business enterprise.

    Intangible assets and intellectual property are the *soft* assets of a company as listed in Figure #2. Generally, intellectual properties are those created by the law. Trademarks, patents, copyrights and trade secrets are some of the examples listed as intellectual property in Figure #2. Intangible assets are of a similar nature. They often do not possess a physical embodiment but are nonetheless still very valuable to the success of a business. Customer lists, distribution networks, union contracts and company practices are among the assets listed as intangible assets.

45

All of the assets of the business enterprise framework contribute to the revenue and profit-generating capability of the business. They are also the underlying basis for the value of the business as depicted in Figure #3. The equity and long-term debt values represent the basis by which all other assets of a company were acquired, whether by purchase or internal creation.

Figure #2			
Business = Enterprise	Working Capital +	Fixed Capital +	Intangible Assets & Intellectual Property
	- Inventory - Cash - Accounts Receivable - Mineral Reserves	- Offices - Warehouses - Manufacturing - Research Labs	- Patents - Trademarks - Copyrights - Know-how - Designs - Formulae - Trade Secrets - Distribution Networks - Supply Contracts - Subscribers - Franchises - Licenses - Customer Lists - Practices - Work Force - Union Contracts - Research Capabilities

Figure #3 also shows that the value of the same enterprise, as depicted in Figures #1 and #2, equals the value of the aggregate asset categories. The value of the enterprise is equal to the present value of the equity of the stock of the company and the long-term debt of the company. These two components are also referred to as the invested capital of the company.

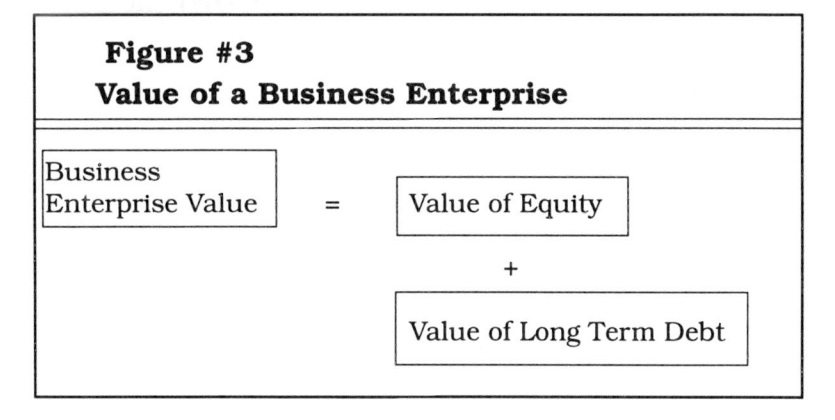

Figure #3
Value of a Business Enterprise

Business Enterprise Value = Value of Equity
+
Value of Long Term Debt

All of the assets comprising the business enterprise framework contribute to the commercialization of intellectual property by allowing for the creation and delivery of products or services which generate revenues and profits for a company. The ability of a company to sustain earnings makes it a valuable investment.[2] The relative value of intellectual property can be identified by estimating the portion of value or earnings attributed to specific intellectual property. Figure #4 shows that the profits of an enterprise can be allocated to the different asset categories that comprise the enterprise. The amount of profits enjoyed by an enterprise is directly related to the existence of the different asset categories. Companies lacking any one category of assets would have different profits. The earnings of a business are derived from exploiting its

---

[2] Earnings are the basis of value. The valuation of corporate stock is most often based on the present value of the expected future earnings of a company. The amount, growth rate and risks associated with expected earnings is typically converted into a value for the price of a company's stock.

assets. The amount of assets in each category along with the nature of the assets and the quality of the assets determines the level of earnings that the business generates.

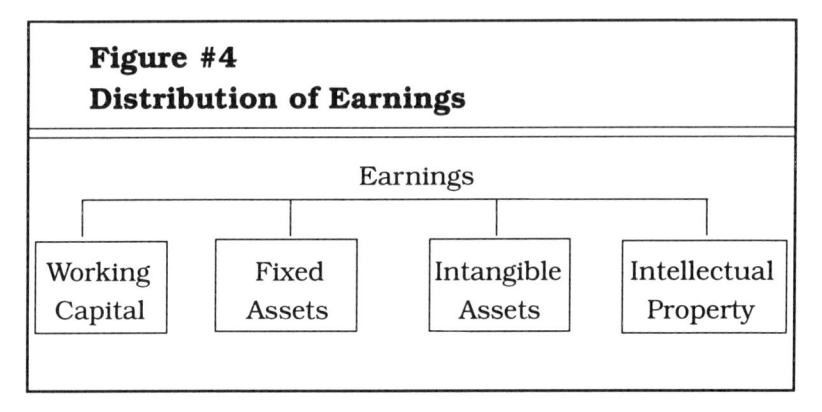

**Figure #4
Distribution of Earnings**

Earnings
- Working Capital
- Fixed Assets
- Intangible Assets
- Intellectual Property

Going Beyond Commodity Earnings

Working capital, fixed assets and intangible assets are arguably commodity assets that all businesses can possess and exploit. A company that possesses only these limited assets will enjoy only limited earnings because of the competitive nature of commodities. A company that generates superior earnings must have something special, usually in the form of intellectual properties such as patented technology, trademarks or copyrights.

Excess earnings generally occur in three primary ways:

1. Price premiums are charged and obtained from the sale of technology-based products where the marketplace is willing to pay a higher price than it otherwise would be expected to pay for products lacking the technologically-based enhancement of utility. When all, or a portion, of the premium survives manufacturing costs and operating expenses, the enhanced bottomline profit margins are considered to be directly

attributed to the existence of unique technology or other intellectual property.

2. When a technology allows for a product or service to be produced and/or delivered at a reduced cost, the enhanced earnings are attributed to the technology used in the operations.

3. Expanded market share can also generate incrementally higher profit margins from economies of scale that come from high volume production. This can occur even when premium product pricing or manufacturing cost savings are not possible.

Gravel quarries are generally an excellent example of a commodity business. The product delivered by quarries lacks the enhanced utility introduced by technological intellectual property. These companies possess all of the typical business enterprise asset categories previously discussed except for intellectual property. They may even possess extensive amounts of intangible assets in the form of customer lists, corporate procedures and favorable union contracts. Yet the nature of their product places gravel quarries in a very competitive position where excess earnings beyond those obtainable in a commodity business are not sustainable for the long-term. Overall, profit margins in the quarry business are slim because of the absence of intellectual property for which the company can charge premium prices.

Later in this chapter the allocation of earnings among the asset categories of the business enterprise (see Figure #4) is demonstrated as a foundation for deriving royalty rates. The allocation is based on each asset category earning a fair rate of return on the investment value of the category. When the profits of the company are *absorbed* by the investment rate of return requirements of working capital, fixed assets and intangible assets, then minimal amounts of earnings are available for allocation to intellectual property. Such is often the case in a gravel quarry business enterprise. In other industries, substantial amounts of earnings are still available after the rate of return requirements of non-technological assets are satisfied. The excess amount of earnings is derived from the existence of intellectual property. In many cases, technology is the driving force.

Stock portfolios are illustrative of this concept. A portfolio of stocks can be compared to the composition of a business enterprise. Instead of working capital, fixed assets, intangible assets and intellectual property, a comparative stock portfolio might be comprised of bank stocks, equipment leasing company stocks, business service stocks and technology stocks. The total return of the portfolio is derived from the different stocks. The value of the different stocks is directly related to the portion they deliver to the total portfolio return.[3] In the case of stock portfolios, the total return is calculated by adding the returns provided by the different stocks in the portfolio. The separate returns of each component of the portfolio are known. This is not the case for the *business enterprise portfolio.* The total earnings of the business enterprise is the known quantity and the allocation among the contributing components is the objective for quantifying the value of intellectual property and establishing a subset of business profits to allocate to licensed technology as a royalty.

---

[3] The investment risk associated with the individual stock returns is also an important valuation concept that will be discussed later in this chapter.

Market Approach

Market transactions that directly indicate intellectual property values are hard to discover, but on April 2, 1993 an excellent example played out. In an attempt to halt market share advances by generic discount cigarettes, Philip Morris announced on April 2, 1993 a twenty percent price cut of its premier MARLBORO brand cigarette. Discount cigarettes have demonstrated substantial growth, as poor economic conditions have caused many beleaguered consumers to question the price-to-value equation associated with products that have brand images but commodity-like characteristics. Discount cigarettes have captured almost thirty-six percent of the market from a standstill start in 1981. Some analysts estimate that discount cigarettes may achieve a fifty percent market share by the end of the decade. The price differential between generic and branded cigarettes prior to April 2, 1993 was a substantial $1.40 per pack. Generics could be found at some stores for $1.00 while premium branded cigarettes like MARLBORO commanded a retail price of $2.40 per pack. Philip Morris decided that narrowing this price differential could slow the advancing market share of generic cigarettes. Wall Street analysts estimated that the price cut would reduce the pre-tax tobacco earnings of Philip Morris by $2 billion from the $5.2 billion it earned in the prior fiscal year. The announcement was met by heavy stock trading which forced the stock price of Philip Morris down by twenty-three percent in one day. The closing price on April 2 represented a one-day loss in value of $13 billion, all of which can be considered as a reduction in the value of the MARLBORO trademark. Extrapolation of this event can be used to get an indication of value for the MARLBORO brand. The $13 billion might be looked on as twenty percent of the value of the brand before the price cut. Therefore, the brand had a value of $65 billion before April 2 and $52 billion afterward. The MARLBORO brand still commands a premium price over generic products and still retains a large number of loyal consumers, but the upper boundary of price at which consumers are willing to pay for image and mystique has been found.

Another unique opportunity was presented by VLI Corporation for valuing a patent. The activities of the company, for the most part, were based on one patented product. The product was the TODAY brand vaginal contraceptive sponge. Sales reached $17 million in 1986 from a standstill in 1983. The product was stocked in more than ninety-three percent of all drugstores nationwide and in eighty-eight percent of all food stores that carry contraceptives. During September 1987, the company reported that the U.S. Patent and Trademark Office denied the company's petition to reinstate the expired patent on the sponge. The original patent expired in July because the company failed to pay a then, newly-required patent maintenance fee on time. While the missed payment was called "inadvertent" by the company, the Patent Office did not renew the patent. The company was, at the time, a takeover target of American Home Products Corporation, which offered $7 in July 1987 for each of VLI's 11.9 million shares. This was contingent upon reinstatement of the patent. This represented a value for the company of $83.3 million. As of October 1987, the shares were trading over-the-counter at $4 per share. Typically, a takeover candidate trades at the price offered by the suitor and many times at a price slightly higher. The premium, above

Valuing Patents and Technology for Licensing / Four

the offer price, represents speculation that another buyer may materialize with an offer of a higher amount. In this case, the stock was trading below the $7 offer. The $3 difference can be viewed as the value of the patent protection. When multiplied by the number of shares, the value of the patent equaled $35.7 million. The market concluded that the same company, with the same product and the same distribution system, while serving the same market, was worth substantially less without the patent. The protection against competitive copying was lost. As a result, competitive products could almost immediately be introduced. VLI could experience pricing pressures and a loss in sales volume. In consideration of this possibility, the market dropped the share price of the company. Another way to express the value of the patent would be to calculate the present value of all earnings that will be lost due to the entrance of competition. In this case, the market indirectly made that calculation with the lower stock price reflecting the potentially lost earnings. The $3 difference may actually undervalue the patent. Somewhere within the considerations the market used to price the shares at $4 was the probability that the patent would eventually be reinstated.

VLI said that company attorneys assured them that there would not be any trouble getting the patent reinstated. This is one of the first times that a patent expired due to failure by a company to make a patent maintenance fee payment. The Patent Office may or may not stick to its new procedures. If it becomes clear that reinstatement will not be granted, the price of the stock could drop further. The company is still valued at $47.6 million because it can still sell the sponge product, but it is now subject to more direct competition by "copycat" sponges. In addition, the company does have other products, but they are presently of only minor importance. The market has set the value of the patented TODAY contraceptive sponge at $35.7 million.

The Scarcity of Market Data

The exchange of intellectual property in the marketplace is typically completed as part of the exchange of an entire company or division. Rarely do we see a specific patent or trademark exchanged as an independent entity. Usually, the exchange includes the enterprise with which the intellectual property is associated. The price paid for the enterprise includes an amount for working capital, fixed assets, the assembled work force and various types of intangible assets and intellectual property. Even where specific intellectual properties are exchanged separately, the price is rarely disclosed. Some recent instances where intellectual property has traded independently and where price information was disclosed include:

- the sale of the AFTER SIX trademark as part of a bankruptcy liquidation for $7 million;
- the purchase of the patented Polymerase Chain Reaction technology from Cetus Corporation by Roche Holdings Ltd. for $300 million plus five years of royalties;
- the purchase of seven liquor trademarks by American Brands, Inc. from Seagram Company for $372.5 million. (The marks included CALVERT GIN, CALVERT EXTRA AMERICAN WHISKEY, KESSLER AMERICAN BLENDED WHISKEY, LEROUX COCKTAILS, LORD

CALVERT CANADIAN WHISKEY, RONRICO RUM and WOLFSCHMIDT VODKA.);
- the sale of the BLACK HAWK trademark in 1985 for $3 million as part of the bankruptcy of Rath Company, a meat packer;
- the sale of the GLORIA VANDERBILT trademark by Murjani in 1988 for $15 million to Gitano;
- the purchase of thirty-two medical remedy trademarks by Menley & James Laboratories for $52 million.

Combined sales for the brand names purchase by American Brands totaled $235 million for the fiscal year just prior to the transaction. A simple market multiple can be calculated indicating a price-to-revenue multiple of 1.59 for "middle brow" liquor brands. Without possessing more detailed product information from Seagram, only simplistic allocations of purchase price can be accomplished. Still, if the total price is divided equally among the seven names, then the value of each brand is approximately $53.2 million. Since the brand name CALVERT is used in three of the names purchased, it might be more appropriate to divide the purchase price by four yielding a per brand value of $93.1 million.

The thirty-two trademarks purchased by Menley & James included over-the-counter medical remedies such as CONTAC cold remedy, ECOTRIN aspirin, HOLD cough medicine, ARM allergy medicine and ROSEMILK skin lotion. Combined annual sales of all thirty-two trademarked products just prior to the purchase were $30 million, indicating a price-to-revenue multiple of 1.73 for the trademarks. On a per-name basis, the value per trademark equals $1.6 million. Menley & James uses contract manufacturing, warehousing and distribution. All that was purchased were the marks.

The market approach provides an indication of value by comparing the price at which similar property has exchanged between willing buyers and sellers. When the market approach is used, an indication of the value of a specific item of intellectual property can be gained from looking at the prices paid for comparable property. Requirements for successful use of this approach include:

- an active market involving comparable property;
- past transactions of comparable property;
- access to price information at which comparable property exchanged; and
- arm's length transactions between independent parties.

The most difficult aspect of the market approach as it applies to intellectual property is comparability. Even if pricing information for a specific exchange regarding a specific patent or trademark were available, the price at which the property exchanged most likely will have no bearing on the value of other patents and trademarks unless positive comparability exists.

Comparability

In residential real estate, comparability is quite easy. The neighborhood, square footage, number of rooms and quality of construction can all be compared to the indications of value established by past sales of other homes. Adjustments can be made for differences such as pools, fireplaces and finished basements. After adjustments, the market transactions can lead to a value for the house being studied. Unfortunately, valuation by the market approach is not as easy for intellectual properties such as patents and trademarks. Many factors come into play. Presented below are some of the most important factors that should be considered when seeking intellectual property comparability:

- Industry
- Market Share
- Profits
- New Technologies
- Barriers to Entry
- Growth Prospects
- Legal Protection
- Remaining Economic Life

The value of a business enterprise, including all of the tangible and intangible assets, is greatly influenced by the industry in which the property is used. Industry cycles and economics can limit the value of businesses and the intellectual property that they possess. Market transactions that are to serve as a basis for an indication of value are most useful if the exchanged property is employed within the same industry and subject to the same prospects, demographic factors, government regulation and investment risks. If a trademark used in the cosmetics industry were sold, the price at which the transaction occurred might be a good indication of the value of other cosmetic trademarks. This assumes, however, that the influence of the other factors listed is the same. A trademark that was exchanged in the steel industry would not be considered useful for valuing a cosmetics trademark.

Profitability is fundamental to the existence of monetary value. Intellectual property that contributes to strong and continuing profits is very valuable. Market transactions involving trademarks in the same industry might not be a reasonable comparable unless profitability measures are the same. An excellent example is the sports products industry. For the most part, the primary players in the sport shoe market manufacture products of almost equal quality. Each competitor has products with designs and features that are intended to enhance athletic performance and prevent injury. Yet some branded products have achieved substantial profits above the average achieved by major competitors. Part of this should be attributed to the recognizability of the trademarks by consumers and the positive attributes that they associate with the name. If a sport shoe trademark were to exchange, an indication of value for another trademark in the same industry might not necessarily be provided, unless the profits associated with the trademark were at similar levels. While industry transactions are a fundamental factor for judging comparability, comparable profitability is also important.

Market share can sometimes be associated with profitability. Control of a large share of a big market naturally provides a company with enhanced profits. Patented products and trademarks can contribute to maintenance of a significant market share, and this factor must be reflected in the value of intellectual property. Intellectual property transactions may not be comparable if the market share comparisons are not positive.

Emerging technologies can have a significant impact on the value of intellectual property. New emerging technologies represent increased competition, which can affect the remaining life of intellectual property. When looking at intellectual property transactions as market indications of value, care must be taken to assure that the effect of emerging technology is comparable with the property being valued. The existence of research that is expected to make the subject property obsolete must be reflected in the value decision.

Barriers to entry can enhance the value of intellectual property. Barriers include distribution networks, substantial capital investments, and well-entrenched competitors. FDA approval in the drug industry is an example of a barrier to entry. The value of currently accepted proprietary drug products is supported, in a sense, by the hurdles that competitors must jump in order to enter the market. The time delay allows the current products to enjoy less competition, higher pricing options and most importantly, an opportunity to dominate the market. As such, intellectual property within a market that also presents high entry-barriers is possibly more valuable than similar property that operates in a more open industry.

Growth prospects are directly related to value. This relationship exists because a growing income stream is more valuable than a flat or declining income stream. The intellectual property that the income stream flows from is valued according to the growth prospects of the income. Generally, higher growth can be associated with higher value, assuming that investment risks are the same. Comparable market transactions are not useful as value indicators if the properties being compared have decidedly different prospects for future income growth.

Intellectual property values are derived from the legal protection that excludes others from making use of the property. When there is a question about the strength of this protection, the value of intellectual property is weakened. This is especially true for patents. A basic patented technology covering the activities for an entire industry is far more valuable than a patent covering a small aspect of an industry. If a patented technology can be "designed around," then the underlying value of the patent is weak. Evidence of value can usually be detected in the number of industry participants lining up to take licenses at royalties that leave little room for negotiation.

Remaining life must also be considered in the valuation of intellectual property. Two patents with many similar characteristics of industry application, growth potential, profits and market share may still not be reasonable comparisons if one has only a few years until expiration.

When market transactions of specific intellectual property exist that have similar characteristics to the property under study, direct application of the market approach is possible. When intellectual property has been exchanged as part of a package of assets (usually as part of a business enterprise), then an allocation of the purchase price among the assets is required in order to identify the amount that is specifically attributable to the intellectual property.

Market transaction information is slightly more common for licensing. Royalty rates at which different types of technology have been licensed can be discovered and used in pricing new technology. Attention should be given to the eight factors previously discussed to make sure the market-derived royalty rates represent the price at which comparable property has exchanged.

Royalty Rate Determination Methods

Underlying the following discussion is the idea that intellectual property is an investment asset. Licensing strategies often seek to gain the highest rate of return on intellectual properties. As such, royalty rates should reflect the same factors that drive the rate of return requirements associated with all other business assets.

Market Transactions In General And On Average

Information about royalty rates obtained by others in third-party market transactions can show a *typical* royalty rate for an industry, but as this analysis will show, a more precise model is still needed. The bar chart presented in Figure #5 summarizes royalty rates associated with technology licenses.[4] A total of 95 licenses are represented involving technology transfers in the telecommunications, semiconductor and computer industries. The answer to the question — *What is a typical royalty rate for advanced technology?* — can be addressed from an analysis of the charted data.

The average royalty rate, weighted by the number of times it showed up in a license agreement, is 5.1 percent. If the high end royalty rates of twenty

---

[4] The information for this analysis was generously provided by Michael Merwin of Ernst & Young, Chicago, Illinois and *Licensing Economics Review*, Moorestown, New Jersey

and thirty percent are eliminated as being anomalies, then the weighted average royalty rate is four percent. Based on this analysis, some negotiators are happy to finalize their agreements using a royalty rate of four or five percent. By using this information, we are assuming that the technology we are attempting to quantify is reasonably comparable to the technology involved in the 95 licenses analyzed. The problem is that a specific technology cannot be comparable to all of the 95 licensed technologies. It can only be similar to some of the transferred technology. As such, the market transaction royalty rates should mostly be looked on as general guidance that helps to define the boundaries within which a settlement royalty rate should fall.

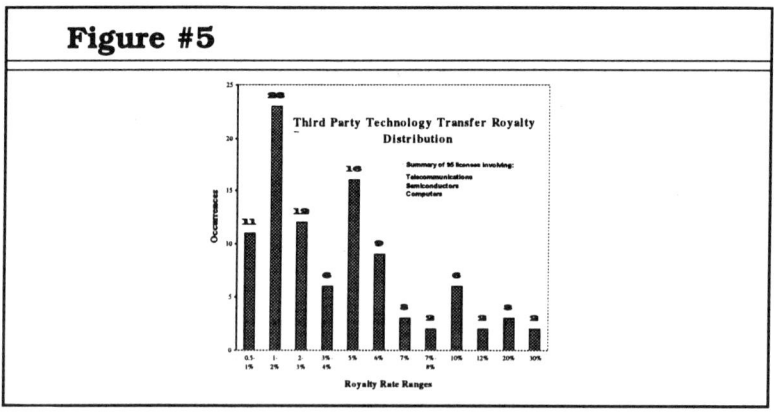

Figure #5

The most frequently reported royalty rate was five percent. It was found in sixteen of the 95 licenses. The second most frequently negotiated royalty rate was two percent which was found in fourteen agreements. Third place went to three percent, with appearances in eleven licenses. The fourth most frequently negotiated rate was six percent. It showed up nine times. Fifth place went to royalty rates of 1.5 percent with eight appearances. A royalty rate of one percent showed up seven times. The table below, Figure #6, summarizes the frequency of the most common rates.

Figure #6
Bar Chart Data: Most Common Royalty Rates

Royalty Rate	Frequency
5.0%	16
2.0%	14
3.0%	11
6.0%	9
1.5%	8
1.0%	7

Our analysis now shows us the average royalty rates negotiated and the number of times specific rates were negotiated. A cumulative analysis provides additional insights:

- 55 percent of the licenses involved royalty rates of four percent or less.
- 72 percent of the licenses involved royalty rates of five percent or less.
- 81 percent of the licenses involved royalty rates of six percent or less.
- 93 percent of the licenses involved royalty rates of ten percent or less.
- 95 percent of the licenses involved royalty rates of twelve percent or less.

In this analysis, we have developed a general range of reasonable royalty rates. However, something is missing from the analysis: something that will allow the market information just presented to be filtered for direct application to a specific technology reflecting specific conditions. We are missing a model that will focus on earning fair rates of return on the investments committed to the project.

An investment rate of return model can yield a royalty rate that allows the licensor to earn a fair rate of return on his or her investment in the project while returning to the licensee a royalty reflecting the value of the licensed technology and its contribution to the success of the contemplated project. An investment rate of return model that allows a licensee to earn a fair rate of return on his or her investment in the project is key to filtering the market data. The model must consider the working capital committed to the project. Also considered must be the investment in fixed assets such as manufacturing facilities. Additionally, the model should provide the licensee with a fair rate of return on the investment value of the intangible assets and intellectual property they are contributing to the project such as complementary patents, trademarks, customer lists and distribution networks. Such a model is presented later in this chapter.

Rules-of-Thumb that Don't Work

Market transactions and rules-of-thumb leave a lot to be desired. Previously negotiated royalty rates are often relied upon for setting royalties in new license transactions. But there are a lot of problems with comparability. Rules-of-thumb are popular but they are of questionable heritage. Where did they come from and what is their basis?

Some of the more commonly used royalty rate development methods are discussed in this section of the chapter. They are attractive because of their simplicity. The methods are popular because of their universal application. They are easy to understand and use. In most cases, however, they should be avoided.

The "25%" Rule

This method calculates a royalty as twenty-five to $33^1/_3$ percent of the gross profit, before taxes, from the enterprise operations in which the licensed intellectual property is used. At best, this method of royalty determination is crude. Gross profit has never been accurately defined where this rule is discussed. Gross profits, based on generally accepted accounting principle definitions, reflect the direct costs of production-manufacturing expenses. These include raw material costs, direct labor costs, utility expenses and even the depreciation expenses of the manufacturing facilities. All of the costs and expenses associated with conversion of raw materials into a final product or service are captured in the gross profit figure. Since this is often the area of greatest contribution from intellectual property, consideration of the amount of gross profits is reasonable. It fails, however, to consider the final profitability that is ultimately realized from the intellectual property. Absent from the analysis are operating expenses such as sales, administrative and general overhead expenses. An argument for eliminating operating expenses from the analysis might center on the idea that the value of intellectual property, such as manufacturing technology, is best measured by the enhancement of profits in the area of the business in which the technology has the most direct effect. A more broadened view shows that royalties can be affected by selling expenses and operating expenses that are part of the commercialization.

Intellectual property that is part of a product or service which requires small amounts of marketing, advertising and selling effort is far more valuable than a product based upon intellectual property that requires huge efforts in these areas. When national advertising campaigns, highly compensated sales personnel and highly skilled technical support people are needed to provide customer support, bottomline profits are lowered. Two patented products may cost the same amount to produce and yield the same amount of gross profit. Yet one of the products may require extensive and continuing sales support. The added costs of extensive and continuing sales efforts make the first product less profitable to the licensee. While the two products may have the same gross profit margins, it is very unlikely that they would command the same royalty given the different assumptions about selling and support costs.

The operating profit level, after consideration of the non-manufacturing operating expenses, is a far more accurate determinant of the contribution of the intellectual property. The royalty for specific intellectual property must reflect the industry and economic environment in which the property is used. Some environments are competitive and require a lot of support, which reduces net profits. Intellectual property that is used in this type of environment is not as valuable as intellectual property in a high profit environment where less support costs are required. A proper royalty must reflect this aspect of the economic environment in which it is to be used. A royalty based on gross profits alone cannot reflect this reality.

The percentage of gross profit that should ultimately go to the licensor is considered by most advocates of The 25% Rule to be flexible. Yet when a licensee must heavily invest in complementary assets, a lower percentage of gross profit may be more proper. If very little investment is needed, then a royalty based on a larger share of gross profits may go to the licensor. Intuitively, this is correct, yet the methodology provides no clues as to quantifying a relationship between licensee capital investment and the percentage of gross profit that goes to royalty.

The 25% Rule also fails to consider the other key royalty determinants of risk and fair rates of return on investment. Higher risk rates generally indicate lower investment values. Lower investment values mean that lower royalty rates are indicated. A royalty method focusing on gross profits does not even begin to capture the risk that is associated with the business in which the intellectual property is used.

The Industry Norms Method

This royalty rate determination methodology misses even more of the important elements than The 25% Rule. The Industry Norm method focuses on the rates that others are charging for intellectual property licensed within the same industry. Investment risks, net profits, market size, growth potential and complementary asset investment requirements are all absent from direct consideration. The use of Industry Norms places total reliance on the ability of others to correctly consider and interpret the many factors affecting royalties. It places total reliance on the abilities of the founders of the Industry Norm rate. Any mistakes made by the initial setting of an industry royalty are passed along.

Changing economic conditions along with changing investment rate of return requirements also are absent from consideration when using this method. A royalty established only a few years ago is probably inadequate for reflecting the changes in the value of the licensed property and the changes that have occurred in the investment marketplace. Even if an industry norm royalty rate was a fair rate of return at the time it was established, there is no guarantee that it is still valid. Value, economic conditions, rates of return and all of the other factors that drive a fair royalty have dynamic properties. They constantly change and so must the underlying analysis that establishes royalties.

The Return on R&D Costs Method

When determining a reasonable royalty, the amount spent on development of the intellectual property is a terribly attractive factor to consider. Unfortunately, development costs are also terribly misleading. The amount spent in the development is rarely equal to the value of the property. A proper royalty should provide a fair return on the value of the asset regardless of the costs incurred in development.

The underlying value of intellectual property is founded on the amount of future economic benefits that are expected to be derived from commercialization of the property. The development costs do not reflect these benefits in any way, shape or form.

The U.S. Government spent many millions on development of nuclear powered aircraft engines in the 1950's. Engines were tested and prototypes were built. Development costs soared. Unfortunately, nuclear powered engines were never able to deliver the thrust needed to get aircraft airborne. As such, the value of nuclear aircraft engine technology would appropriately be considered low: zero. But, a determination based on development costs would indicate a high royalty because future economic benefits are not a factor.

The Return on Sales Method

A royalty that is based on net profits as a percentage of revenues has several primary weaknesses. The first difficulty is determination of the proper allocation of the profits between the licensor and the licensee. A precise and quantifiable method for dividing the net profits is rarely specified when this royalty rate methodology is used. Another area of weakness is the lack of consideration for the value of the intellectual property that is invested in the enterprise as well as a lack of consideration for the value of the complementary monetary and tangible assets that are invested. Finally, this method fails to consider the relative investment risk associated with the intellectual property.

The 5% of Sales Method

For unknown reasons, one of the most popular royalty determination methods is to calculate five percent of sales — sales multiplied by .05 equals royalty payment. It shows up in a lot of different industries. It is associated with embryonic technology and mature trademarks. It has been found in the food, industrial equipment, electronics, construction and medical device industries. Forget profits, capital investment, earnings growth, operating expenses, investment risk and even development costs. Somehow five percent of sales prevails. Don't be fooled. It's not a magic bullet answer. It doesn't consider any of the factors discussed in this chapter.

Complex Factors That Can Impact Royalty Rates

The primary reason that a general rule-of-thumb fails is because too many important factors, specific to the technology and industry under study, cannot be reflected by simplified rules. Listed below are some of the complex factors that should be reflected in technology pricing. Three primary factors are identified along with a subset of factors for each of the primary ones. Other methods exist that can alleviate part of the problems associated with rules-of-thumb, and they will be described in the remainder of this chapter.

- Economic Benefits Derived From The Technology
    - benefits derived from complementary assets
    - competitor efforts impacting the economic benefits
    - consumer reactions
    - management competency
    - production efficiencies
    - commercialization expenses
    - commercialization time frame requirements
- Duration Of The Economic Benefits
    - rapid technological obsolescence
    - alternate technologies
    - validity of patent risks
    - changing consumer reactions
- Risk Of Receiving The Economic Benefits
    - economic risk
    - regulatory risk
    - political risk
    - inflationary risk
    - unexpected conditions and events

Infringement Damages Analysis

The strength of patents allow patent owners to negotiate higher royalties. The new and favorable attitude toward patents originated in the Carter Administration and came to fruition in 1981. The patent system was fundamentally strengthened with the creation of The Court of Appeals of the Federal Circuit (CAFC), which is the only court that handles intellectual property-based appeals throughout the nation. Its decisions have clarified and made uniform U.S. law.

Previous to 1981, when infringement cases were initiated, preliminary injunctions were granted only when there was a reasonable likelihood that the infringed patent could be proved to be valid and infringed. While preliminary injunctions were typically granted in trademark and copyright cases, they were seldom granted for patents. The owner of the infringed patent was required to prove the validity of the patent in order to be granted a preliminary injunction. Only where prior court decisions had found the patent valid was this really possible. Therefore, injunctions were rarely granted for patent cases. To infringe on an existing patent was not a risky decision because an infringer could continue to exploit an infringing product or service while the court case dragged out. In cases where infringement was decided, damage awards were typically expressed as royalties in amounts that represented what would have been negotiated had the infringer taken a license before beginning the infringing activity. Prior to the creation of the CAFC, infringement was almost a risk-free strategy. The worst consequence an infringer faced was payment of the low royalty that should have been initially negotiated.

Currently, the CAFC standard has placed the burden of proving a patent invalid upon the infringer. This supports the patent owner. Infringers must provide clear and substantial proof of invalidity; otherwise, the patent owner is considered to have a valid patent. This attitude of presumed validity is very powerful and makes infringement very costly and risky. Entire manufacturing plants may be shut down and entire work forces may be indefinitely on layoff. Substantial investments by infringers can be rendered worthless, making infringement more costly than ever. This new attitude by the CAFC strengthens our patent system, making patents more valuable than ever before. Another shift in the legal system that enhances patent values is the willingness of juries to grant huge awards. Where willful infringement is proven, the damage award can be increased to three times the actual amount of damages.

Legal protection of intellectual property is not at all limited to the United States. Germany, Great Britain, Japan and France are all providing strong legal protection for intellectual property. Argentina is in the midst of reforming intellectual property laws, as are The Peoples Republic of China, South Korea, Taiwan, the former Soviet Union and many other developing nations that wish to fully participate in the global economy.

Infringement Damages: The Analytical Approach

The analytical approach is a method for deriving a reasonable royalty, first expressed in a patent infringement court decision. While a license negotiation may be independent of any legal actions, insight can be gained from considering the royalty rate models that are used in legal proceedings. The analytical approach, as dubbed by the courts, determines a reasonable royalty as the difference between profits expected from infringing sales and a normal industry profit level. The analytical approach can be summarized by the following equation:

$$\text{Expected Normal Profit Margin} - \text{Profit Margin} = \text{Royalty Rate}$$

In *TWM Mfg. Co., Inc. v. Dura Corp.*, 789 F.2d 895, 899 (Fed. Cir. 1986), a royalty for damages was calculated based on an analysis of the business plan of the infringer prepared just prior to the onset of the infringing activity. The court discovered the profit expectations from using the infringed technology from internal memorandums written by top executives of the infringing company. Internal memorandums showed that company management expected to earn gross profit margins of almost 53 percent from the proposed infringing sales. Operating profit margins were then calculated by subtracting overhead costs to yield an expected profit margin of between 37 and 42 percent. To find the portion of this profit level that should be provided as a royalty to the plaintiff, the court considered the standard, normal profits earned in the industry at the time of infringement. These profit levels were determined to be between 6.6 and twelve 12.5 percent. These normal industry profits were considered to represent profit margins that would be acceptable to firms operating in the industry. The remaining thirty percent of profits were found to represent a reasonable royalty from which to calculate infringement damages. On appeal the Federal Circuit affirmed.

Normal Industry Profits

A problem with the analytical approach centers on answering the question, *What's a normal industry profit margin?* Normal is hard to quantify. It is meant to reflect the profit margins that might be gained from operating the businesses in an industry absent the technology in question. It can also be difficult to find agreement on what constitutes normal profit margins for an individual company. Different subsidiaries, divisions and even different product lines within the same company can display wide swings in profitability. Many large companies have a portfolio of businesses. Some of the product offerings are mature products which enjoy large market shares but contribute only moderate profit margins because of selling price competition. Other product offerings are emerging products that have great potential for profits and market share but won't deliver earnings contribution until a later date. Still other products of the same diversified company might contribute huge profits because of a technological advantage but only from exploitation of a small market niche.

A More Comprehensive Analytical Approach

Exploitation of intellectual property requires the integration of different types of resources and assets. Intellectual property by itself rarely spews forth money. The equation of commercialization requires working capital, fixed assets, intangible assets and intellectual property. A more comprehensive version of the analytical approach should be utilized —enhanced to the extent that the profits to be allocated between the licensor and licensee reflect the dynamic relationship between profits and the amounts invested in the complementary assets.

A company that produces a commodity product is by definition in a competitive environment. The product price is impacted by heavy competition, and profits margins are thin. In such an environment, an efficient market will eventually stabilize the pricing of the commodity product to a level that allows participants in the market to earn a fair rate of return on the assets invested in the business but no more. A fair return would be earned on the working capital, fixed assets and intangible assets but excess profits are not typically earned from the production and sale of a commodity product.

A company producing an enhanced product, using proprietary technology, possesses elements of product differentiation that allow the producer to charge a premium price. The premium might be due to a trademark that consumers associate with quality. Alternatively, the premium might be derived from special utility offered by the product covered by patented technology. The price premium might even be derived from a combination of trademark and technological advantages. The producer of the enhanced product would earn a profit that represents a fair return on its working capital, fixed assets, intangible assets and an excess return from the intellectual property. The highest amount of royalty that a commodity product producer should be willing to pay to license rights to manufacture and sell the enhanced product is the amount of excess profits associated with the intellectual property. The commodity product licensee would expect to continue to earn a fair rate of return from its investment in working capital, fixed assets and intangible assets.

The investment returns earned by a commodity product manufacturer on the complementary assets used to manufacture and sell the commodity product can be equated to the normal or standard industry profits. When this amount is subtracted from the total returns earned from commercializing the enhanced product, the difference represents the amount contributed by the intellectual property.

The analytical approach can work well when the normal industry profit is derived from analysis of commodity products. The analysis requires that the benchmark commodity profit margin be derived from products competing in the same, or similar, industry as the infringing product, for which a reasonable royalty is being sought. The benchmark profits should also reflect similar investment requirements in complementary assets; similar to those required to exploit the enhanced product which is based on the infringed intellectual property. The following equation can provide a reasonable royalty if the above conditions are met:

Enhanced Product Profit Margin - Commodity Product Profit Margin = Royalty Rate

It is important to reiterate that the commodity product benchmark profit margin must be derived from an analysis of a product that:

1. lacks the intellectual property for which a royalty rate is desired and can therefore be described as a commodity product;
2. participates in the same, or similar, industry in which the subject intellectual property product competes;

3. requires a similar relative amount of investment in complementary assets.

Failure of The Analytical Approach

The analytical approach can fail in instances where the benchmark profit margin that is characterized as *normal* or that of a *commodity* contains elements of profitability attributed to other forms of intellectual property. The analytical approach fails to consider the relationship between relative profit margins and the required investment in complementary assets. Great care is also required when defining a benchmark normalized industry profit margin. An enhanced version of the analytical approach should allocate only the differential profit margins associated with specific intellectual property.

Infringement Damages: Qualitative Factors

Another court case listed the important qualitative factors to look at when deriving a royalty rate for damages. Licensing negotiators can also gain insight from considering the implications of these factors. The courts seek to determine the royalty rate the two parties would have negotiated at the time of infringement had they entered into a hypothetical negotiation. In *Georgia-Pacific Corp. v. United States Plywood Corp.*, 318 F.Supp. 1116, 1120 (1970), the court listed fifteen factors that it considered important for deriving a reasonable royalty. These same factors can also provide useful guidance for licensing negotiations that are not part of a lawsuit. The fifteen factors listed by the court are stated below:

1. the royalties received by the patentee for the licensing of the patent in suit, proving or tending to prove an established royalty;

2. the rates paid by the licensee for the use of other patents comparable to the patent in suit;

3. the nature and scope of the license, as exclusive or non-exclusive; or as restricted or non-restricted in terms of territory or with respect to whom the manufactured product may be sold;

4. the licensor's established policy and marketing program to maintain his patent monopoly by not licensing others to use the invention or by gaining licenses under special conditions designed to preserve that monopoly;

5. the commercial relationship between the licensor and the licensee, such as, whether they are competitors in the same territory in the same line of business, or whether they are inventor and promoter.

6. the effect of selling the patented specialty in promoting sales of other products of the licensee; the existing value of the invention to the licensor as a generator of sales of his non-patented items, and the extent of such derivative or convoyed sales;

7. the duration of the patent and the term of the license;

8. the established profitability of the product made under the patent, its commercial success and its current popularity;

9. the utility and advantage of the patent property over the old modes or devices, if any, that had been used for working out similar results;

10. the nature of the patented invention, the character of the commercial embodiment of it as owned and produced by the licensor and the benefits to those who have used the invention;

11. the extent to which the infringer has made use of the invention and any evidence probative of the value of that use;

12. the portion of the profit or selling price that may be customary in the particular business or in comparable businesses to allow for the use of the invention or analogous inventions;

13. the portion of the realizable profit that should be credited to the invention as distinguished from nonpatented elements, the manufacturing process, business risks, or significant features or improvements added by the infringer;

14. the opinion and testimony of qualified experts; and

15. the amount that a licensor (such as the patentee) and a licensee (such as the infringer) would have agreed upon (at the time the infringement began) if both had been reasonably and voluntarily trying to reach an agreement; that is, that amount which a prudent licensee — who desires, as a business proposition, to obtain a license to manufacture and sell a particular article embodying the patented invention — would have been willing to pay as a royalty and yet be able to make a reasonable profit and which amount would have been acceptable by a prudent patentee who was willing to grant a license.

Two basic elements dominate the list of fifteen considerations: profits and precedents. The focus on precedents looks at the actions of both the potential licensor and licensee with regard to how the specific, or similar, intellectual property has been treated. Past licensing deals are scrutinized along with royalties previously negotiated. The actions of other parties in the same industry with similar property are also useful precedents for determining royalty rates. An analysis of the license agreements of others, with an eye to established royalties, can serve as a benchmark for establishing a royalty rate to use as the basis of a business license.

Profits are the other basic element of reasonable royalties that the fifteen *Georgia-Pacific* factors address. What level of profits have been enjoyed from use of the invention? What amount of sales and market share can be attributed to use of the patented invention? What cost savings result from use of the invention? If the technology is new and yet to be commercialized then the same questions must be answered from the point of view of expected profits, market share and cost savings.

Considering the *Georgia Pacific* Factors

When negotiating royalty rates, a licensor would do well to think about the technology to be licensed in light of the answers to the fifteen questions asked by the *Georgia-Pacific* decision. The answers can help focus royalty rate demands to reflect realistic characteristics about the technology.

Factors 1, 2, 3 and 12 of the *Georgia-Pacific* decision look at rates established in past licenses of the subject technology or similar technology. Consideration must be given to the types of licenses granted with respect to exclusivity, the scope of the license, territorial limitations, advance license fees, sublicensing rights, cross-licensing of other technology, transference of know-how, transference of enabling technology and grant-backs of future technology that the licensee may invent. The terms contemplated in a licensing negotiation determine the usefulness of analyzing the established licenses. When licenses comparable to the one being negotiated are available, a starting point, and maybe ending point, is provided. Established rates are difficult to ignore without the existence of special circumstances.

In Factors 4 and 5 of the *Georgia-Pacific* case, the court said that the unwillingness of a patent owner to grant a license to the infringer at an industry established rate at the time of infringement is a pertinent factor in establishing a reasonable royalty for damages calculations. Licenses between industry competitors can be expensive. Licensors with monopoly positions are not likely to easily part with a key business advantage. Any reluctance by a patent owner to share its monopoly position is most likely only going to be overcome by a higher royalty rate unless the potential licensee has something else of value to offer as a trade or as a cross-license. When negotiations are between competitors, a relatively high royalty rate would be expected to result.

Factor 6 looks at the effect of selling the patented specialty in promoting sales of other products of the licensee. Such additional sales are often called convoyed sales. They represent the sales associated with other products of the licensee that can be expected because of the licensed technology. The convoyed products may not use the licensed technology, but the sales can often be attributed directly to the licensed product. When this condition exists, the licensor is going to expect a healthy royalty rate on the licensed product.

Factor 7 considers the duration of the patent and the term of the license. The remaining life of the patent can have a strong bearing on the royalty rate. The potential licensee has to decide if waiting for the patent to expire is a viable business option. But a patent with a short life can also command a high royalty rate. If the patented invention is vital to the plans of the licensee, then a high royalty rate for a short time might be tolerable.

Factors 8, 9, 10, 11 and 13 look at the established profitability of the product made under the patent, its commercial success, its current popularity, its utility and the advantage of the patented property over the old modes or devices that had been used for working out similar results. This is where a financial analysis is important. The comparative questions to answer are: How much will the licensee make using the technology? How much will the licensee make without access to the technology?

Factor 15 considers the amount that a licensor and a licensee would have agreed on, at the time the infringement began, if both had been reasonably and voluntarily trying to reach an agreement.

Consideration of the various factors provides guidance about whether a higher or lower royalty rate is appropriate for the royalty rate negotiations at hand.

Summary

This chapter on pricing technology has explored the basic foundation of attributing value to technology. It has also presented some of the different methods that can used to derive a royalty rate for use in licensing negotiations. When time is short, some negotiations may have to rely on the weak royalty rate indications provided by the rules-of-thumb discussed. When more time is available, additional derivation methods should be employed. The best results are most likely to come from using as many of the different methods as possible, yielding several different indications that can be considered separately and together.

Five:
Negotiating License Agreements

Once a potential licensor has identified those properties which it believes it can successfully license and has determined the value of these properties, the licensor should start to identify and pursue prospective licensees. At this step, the licensor should develop a "contact list" of potential licensees. In some industries, the list of potential licensees may be well-known. However, it is likely that there are more potential contacts than immediately meet the eye, and the search should not be limited to the obvious prospects. Sources for potential contacts may be found in trade journals and other industry-specific publications. It is also possible to develop names of potential licensees by using industry research guides, which may often be found in public libraries. Most libraries stock a multitude of corporate directories, some of which will categorize potential contacts on an industry-by-industry basis. These directories may also be found on most on-line computer services. Similarly, doing a database search on a system such as NEXIS may uncover additional prospects.

Many licensors prefer not to spend their time and energy finding licensing prospects and decide to use the services of an agent or broker who will present the technology to prospective licensees for a percentage of the revenues received. If a prospective licensor or inventor wishes to go this route, it is important to proceed with caution. There are many unscrupulous "invention" companies who will insist on a significant payment up front in order to review the property and develop a marketing plan to present the invention to the industry. Very often, the "review" consists of a cursory patentability search by a subcontracted patent attorney, while the "marketing plan" is merely an unfocused mass mailing directed at hundreds of companies, whether relevant or not. Some of these companies may even extensively exaggerate the number of inventions they have successfully licensed in order to convince the would-be client to spend more money up front. The number of complaints against some of the more unethical invention companies was high enough to prompt the Federal Trade Commission to bring legal action against them in 1995 for consumer fraud. While this does not mean that all of these companies are untrustworthy, the prospective licensor should be wary of anyone who insists on significant sums of money up front. The majority of legitimate agents and brokers in the technology industry will work on a commission basis and will only expect reasonable expenses to be paid up front. If possible, it is best to deal with only those brokers who are recommended by respected colleagues and whose track record is verifiable. If this is not possible, the licensor should ask for and check references, and request verifiable data concerning the broker's record.

Once prospective licensees have been targeted, they should be contacted individually in order to determine their procedures for reviewing outside inventions, as well as the name of the company's contact person or "gate keeper." The licensor should simultaneously begin preparing a licensing memorandum to send to identified individuals. A licensing memorandum, which can be broadly described as a detailed advertisement of the technology's benefits, should set forth in detail what advantages the technology will bring to the licensee, and how licensees will profit from entering into a license. It is incumbent upon the licensor to first make a candid and realistic analysis of the technology and be truly objective about the potential benefits of the invention. Obviously, in order to command any value at all in the open market, the licensed property must provide the licensee with some competitive advantage over its competitors or offer some improvement. Yet the technology should not be presented with the zeal of a late-night television infomercial, nor should it be surrounded with the common puffery of consumer advertising. Potential licensees are not likely to appreciate claims that cannot be substantiated. In fact, exaggeration of the benefits of the technology or other unsupported claims will more than likely turn the potential licensee away.

In view of the above, the licensor should make a thorough and comprehensive review of the technology to be offered for license. Among the factors to be evaluated are:

- the utility of the technology;
- the extent to which the technology will be protected as a patent and/or trade secret;
- the profitability of the market in the targeted licensed territory;
- a comparison of how the technology will measure up to the current state of the art;
- the anticipated date that competitors will develop "catch up" technology; and

- the costs of implementing the licensed technology and getting the final product to the marketplace.

At the very least, this analysis should give the licensor a realistic picture of the likelihood of success in licensing the technology. It will also enable the licensor to develop a thorough and accurate licensing memorandum and will help the licensor to answer a prospective licensee's questions with candor and confidence.

Drafting the Licensing Memorandum

Armed with the above analysis, the licensor can then draft the licensing memorandum for transmission to prospective licensees. In its simplest terms, the licensing memorandum should be an accurate advertisement highlighting the benefits of the available technology and outlining the reasons the prospective licensee should enter into a license agreement. While the memorandum should not reveal confidential information at this stage, it must provide enough details in order to attract the attention of the prospective licensee's "gate keeper." Further, the licensor should assume that the individual in charge of reviewing outside inventions has little or no background in the scientific discipline of the offered technology, and therefore emphasize the benefits of the available technology in non-technical terms, if at all possible.

The licensing memorandum should provide the potential licensee with sufficient information as to what is being offered, how the prospective licensee will benefit from the technology and what type of arrangement is being proposed (i.e., license, cross license or joint venture). Some licensors have been known to spend considerable time and money in developing licensing memoranda, as they are extremely critical to the overall marketing plan.

The licensing memorandum should contain the following material:

- an introduction of the property being offered for license, and how it relates to the prospect's business;
- a brief description of the licensor, including its history and any information regarding its capitalization which demonstrates that it is not a "fly-by-night" operation;
- a concise, accurate, but non-technical description of the technology being offered for license, including drawings, graphs or photographs which illustrate how the technology may be used;
- the scope of patent/trademark/trade secret protection obtained for the licensed property (including copies of issued patents and/or trademarks), or which the licensor has a reasonable expectation (based upon opinions from counsel) are potentially available;
- a general analysis of the economic benefit which the licensee may expect to achieve through the license; and
- the proposed next step, including the most general business terms of the proposed transaction. This can also set the framework for a face-to-face meeting to more fully discuss the available technology, or set forth the terms under which the prospect might be allowed to test

the property before entering into a full-fledged license agreement.

Included with the license memorandum should be both a standard license agreement and a confidential disclosure agreement. Enclosing a standard license at this stage will give the prospective licensee a starting point for negotiating the business terms of the license and will also help avoid the so-called "battle of the forms" which may later ensue. If the licensor is looking for a joint venture partnership rather than a license, a standard joint venture agreement can be enclosed in lieu of a license agreement.

The Confidential Disclosure Agreement

Of course, the licensor cannot just sit back and wait for the licensee to respond to the licensing memorandum. It is incumbent upon the licensor to follow up each and every communication in an attempt to expedite the licensing process. The licensor's goals are to convince the prospective licensee that it has nothing to lose and everything to gain by either: (a) agreeing to review the technology in greater detail; or (b) allowing the licensor to give a face-to-face presentation of the available technology.

At this point, licensors and inventors who achieve either one of these goals are instructed by their intellectual property attorneys that they should not disclose any further details to the licensing prospect until the prospect has signed a confidential disclosure agreement. A confidential disclosure agreement provides that the receiving party will agree to hold the licensor's idea in confidence and will not use or disclose said idea to any third party for the time specified in the agreement without the prior express written consent of the licensor. A sample confidential disclosure agreement is enclosed in the Appendices.

On the advice of counsel, many prospective licensors will insist that the prospect sign and return a confidential disclosure agreement before disclosing further details regarding the available technology. Some prospects will do so, without complaint. Others, however, will refuse, especially when dealing with an unknown party for fear of being exposed to future litigation. Still others will insist that the licensor sign what is commonly referred to as a "waiver agreement," whereby the licensor affirms that there is no confidential agreement established between the two entities and further specifies that the prospective licensee will assume no obligation to maintain the secrecy of the invention. This enables the prospective licensee to protect itself from accusations and lawsuits which claim that the licensee unlawfully misappropriated an idea from an outside source. Licensees are particularly wary of signing licensor's confidential disclosure agreements because they may be working on a similar project internally at the time of the outside submission. Therefore, the safest way for a company to negate this risk is to simply avoid entering into a confidential relationship with any outside entity, and instead insist that all outside entities waive any claim they might otherwise have against the company.

Some inventors attempt to engage the prospective licensee in a "battle of the disclosure agreements." This is sometimes a futile effort. Getting a large corporation to change its established corporate policy regarding these types of agreements can be very difficult. The simple truth is that the licensor may have no choice but to sign a waiver agreement in order to get to the next step in the licensing process.

In cases where the potential licensee is interested in reviewing the submission, but where neither a confidential disclosure agreement nor a waiver agreement is signed, the licensor should appreciate that there is no confidential relationship between the parties. Therefore, the company has no express obligation to preserve the confidentiality of the submission.

Licensors are often faced with the difficult decision as to how to proceed where the prospective licensee has refused to sign a confidential disclosure agreement. In the end, many novice licensors find themselves willing to take the risk of disclosing the idea under non-confidential terms in order to get to the next step, rather than forsaking a potential opportunity. The risk is, of course, lessened in those instances where the licensor is the owner of an issued United States patent directed to the technology. An *issued* patent vests its owner with the right to preclude others from practicing the patented invention. As previously discussed, patent rights are not enforceable until the patent issues. Therefore, if the invention is the subject of a pending application, the inventor runs the risk that a "patent pending" notice may not scare off an unscrupulous party who may be willing to risk a lawsuit when the patent issues in order to get a jump on the marketplace.

However, the decision to proceed without a signed confidential disclosure agreement may not be an open invitation to steal. Typically, prospective licensees (particularly major corporations) are not in the business of stealing other's properties. Most technology companies rely at least in part on alliances with outside inventors and licensors and on technologies they develop. A company which develops a reputation for unscrupulous behavior with respect to outside submissions would soon find itself alienated from the technology invention community. The best way for licensors to protect themselves is to learn all they can about a prospective licensee and rely upon the integrity of the individual or corporation with whom they are dealing with. Further, licensors should not hesitate to develop a paper trail documenting the nature of the submission and what was discussed during any telephone conversations. If possible, a signed memorandum should also be prepared confirming what may have been discussed or disclosed at any face-to-face meetings and identifying who was in attendance. The licensor should also insist upon a written receipt confirming any materials which are left behind with the prospective licensee for review.

Making an Oral Presentation

In the event that the initial contact is successful and the licensee expresses interest in the technology offered, the licensor may be given the opportunity to make an oral presentation. This is, of course, a significant step and should not be taken lightly. Here, the licensor will have a short period of time in which to convince the prospect's business and technical people that it should enter into a license agreement, which may in turn involve a significant amount of risk and investment. This may be the licensor's best opportunity to make its case, and thus, requires careful preparation on the part of the licensor. The location of this presentation will be determined by the parties, and will vary depending upon any number of logistical factors. It is, however, in the licensor's best interest to have the presentation at its own premises. In that case, the licensor will be able to exercise more control over the presentation and will also have the opportunity to impress the visitors with a tour of its facilities.

The licensor should attempt to anticipate the many questions that the prospect may have and assemble its "team" accordingly. While it is helpful to minimize the number of spokespeople, the licensor should make certain that there are qualified individuals on hand to answer both business and technical questions concerning the licensed property. All designated spokespeople should carefully rehearse the presentation before others in the company, who can, hopefully, ask some of the same questions that the prospective licensee might ask, as well as provide helpful feedback as to the overall quality of the presentation. If the team is unprepared, the presentation will inevitably go poorly.

As noted above, the licensor should anticipate both technical and business questions regarding the licensed property. For example, there will likely be technical questions concerning the effectiveness of the technology, comparability with rival systems and potential regulatory problems. Business-related concerns will likely involve the suitability of the technology for the contemplated licensed territory, the cost of implementing the technology and the extent of profitability in both the long and short term. The licensor's team should also be prepared to answer detailed questions concerning the patentability of the technology and the potential enforceability of any issued patents or those which may issue from pending applications. Similarly, the extent that the licensor will make its trade secrets available in support of the technology is also a likely subject for questions, as is the licensor's ability (and willingness) to make its people available for technical consultations during the term of the proposed license. Finally, the licensor's team should be prepared to answer questions concerning the company's ability to keep the licensed technology current, i.e., its ability (and desire) to produce "next generation" products.

The Evaluation Process

It is not likely that the initial meeting will be conclusive one way or another. In the best of all possible worlds, the prospective licensee would be so impressed by the licensor's presentation that it would sign the license agreement on the spot and write out a big check. However, in today's business climate, even if a licensee is clearly convinced that the technology will be worth millions of dollars in the long run, it would be poor negotiation strategy to simply say so. In such circumstances, the prospect's negotiator, his heart about to jump out of his chest with excitement, might just look the inventor in the face, and quietly murmur, "Hmm, well, this might be something we're interested in, can I have another cup of coffee, please?"

Sometimes the prospective licensee will ask the licensor for time to show it to others at the company and to further evaluate the property. It is also common for the prospect to request that the licensor not show the property to others during this evaluation period, especially if the parties are contemplating an exclusive licensing arrangement or a joint venture. Unfortunately for the inventor, most prospective licensees in the technology industry are reluctant to pay any consideration for the chance to further evaluate the technology. The time necessary for this evaluation will vary greatly depending upon the nature of the technology and its complexity. The prospect may also want to have its own intellectual property counsel review the licensor's patent portfolio or even conduct an independent patentability search. The prospect will need to deeply examine the economic factors of the proposed transaction and determine how the licensed technology will fit into the company's product line. However, as a significant delay could possibly jeopardize the success of the entire licensing program, it is wise to reach a clear understanding as to how long the evaluation period will be, and to what extent the licensor will put its marketing efforts on hold. It is also wise to have a written record signed by both companies confirming the understanding of the parties with respect to the evaluation period, identifying what materials are being given to the licensee for the purpose of its evaluation and specifying the means by which these items will be returned to the licensor at the end of the evaluation period in the event that the parties do not go forward.

In the event that the prospect decides that the technology is of potential benefit to its product line, one of two things will happen. The prospect may contact the licensor and indicate that it would like to enter into an agreement and turn the matter over to its attorneys. Alternatively, the company may need more time to complete its evaluation of the technology and may request an additional evaluation period. The time period will, of course, vary depending upon the nature of the technology. Provided that the time requested by the prospective licensee is reasonable, most licensors are generally willing to be flexible. However, it becomes a more difficult decision when the prospective licensee insists that the licensor continue to refrain from disclosing the technology to others. Many licensors, reluctant to lose other potential business opportunities, may request some sign of good faith, or, at the very least, a clear indication as to when it can expect a definitive decision on the license.

It is always good policy for the prospective licensor to follow up with the prospect on a regular basis during this evaluation period. The licensor should be informed about the status of the evaluation process and should reaffirm its willingness to be cooperative in the event that there may be additional questions. While it is not a good idea to become a thorn in the prospective licensee's side, the licensor has every right to call and inquire about the status of the evaluation.

Option Agreements

If, at the end of the initial evaluation period, the licensee believes there may be some merit to the property, but has not yet completed the evaluation process, he or she may ask for an option to enter into a license agreement. In essence, the option agreement buys time for the licensee for further evaluation of the property. In exchange for more time, the licensee agrees to pay the licensor a non-refundable amount of money, which is negotiated by both parties. The option is analogous to a rental of the licensed property for a fixed period of time. During the option period, the licensor will contractually agree that it will not show the idea to any other company. Both the amount of the option payment and the length of the option period will vary depending upon the industry and the technology involved. Most option periods run between thirty and sixty days, although they can be as long as six months in some instances.

The licensor should remember that granting the option to a prospective licensee does not necessarily mean that it will take a license. At the end of the option period, the company will either return the idea or exercise the option and begin to discuss a license agreement. If the company decides not to exercise its option, the licensor is free to continue marketing the idea to other companies.

In the event that the company decides to proceed with a license agreement, one of the first issues to be decided will be how to handle the option payment. Some licensees will ask the licensor to treat the option payment as an advance against earned royalties, while others will acknowledge that the option payment is a non-recoupable payment which should be handled separately from other payments under the license. Clearly, it is in the licensor's best fiscal interest to have the option payment treated separately.

The option agreement should also specifically define which aspects of the technology are being optioned. At a bare minimum, a detailed description of the property should be included. If appropriate, the specific patents and/or applications should be referenced, or attached to the option agreement. The ultimate goal is to be sufficiently specific so as to permit an impartial party years later to read the option agreement and understand the intentions of the parties.

As noted above, the duration of the option agreement must be precisely defined, although it will vary depending upon the industry. The time frame should be long enough to permit the prospective licensee to complete its evaluation but not so long that the licensor misses the window of opportunity for the invention or technology being optioned. The option agreement should also specifically provide that in the event the prospective licensee decides to exercise the option, the parties will enter into a comprehensive license agreement within a specific period of time (i.e., within thirty days). This will protect the licensor from further foot-dragging on the part of the licensee. If possible at this point, it is also advisable to set forth as many of the business terms of the prospective license, such as the royalty rate and/or advance payments, as can be agreed upon. This will clearly expedite the license negotiations later on. The option should also specify that, in the event the prospective licensee chooses not to exercise its option, it will return all materials relating to the property to the licensor and will neither use the idea nor disclose it to any other party.

Six:
The License Agreement

After weeks or even months of discussions and meetings, the day has finally arrived. The prospective licensee has finally agreed to enter into a license agreement with the inventor of the technology. The next step is to hammer out the terms of a license agreement.

The initial negotiations for a license agreement are typically conducted among and between the licensing executives. While there are occasions where one or both parties are accompanied by their attorneys, the presence of counsel is usually reserved for the larger transactions. Where the licensing executives are experienced and the issues are relatively straightforward, there is really no need to involve counsel at this point. The purpose of the initial negotiation is to arrive at some consensus relative to the business terms of the license agreement. There will be sufficient time later on for the lawyers to flesh out the agreement.

The negotiation of a license agreement is consistent with most other business negotiations. Typically, one party is in a better bargaining position than the other. One party might have a stronger incentive to enter into the license than the other and that will usually shift the bargaining leverage to the other party. In negotiating license agreements, leverage is not normally about money. Leverage more commonly involves a party's need to enter into the agreement. That need can be caused by a variety of factors. One party might have a burning desire to enter a particular market, and the license is the means to enter it. One party might desperately need the technology or patents to keep up with its competitors. A party might believe that the license offers it the ability to exclude a competitor from the marketplace. There might even be a hidden agenda in these negotiations. Whatever the motivation, it is rare that both parties have the same leverage.

At this point, it is important to note that there are a myriad of ways to structure a technology transfer agreement. The license agreement is simply one of a number of different alternatives, and the initial negotiation of the final agreement is the time to explore the different alternatives. For example, both parties should explore the possibilities of an outright assignment of the patents and/or technology, or even a possible joint venture. While this is not meant to imply in any way that a license agreement is the least favorable form of technology transfer, the parties should only enter into a license agreement after they are convinced that it is the best vehicle to accomplish their respective goals.

Upon reaching the conclusion that a license agreement is, indeed, the best way to proceed, the first question to be answered is: what should be included in the agreement? Will it be for one or a number of patents? What about foreign patents? Will technology be included and, if so, what technology? Will there be improvements and, if so, who will own them? What are the respective responsibilities of the parties? The breadth or narrowness of the eventual agreement will flow directly from these initial negotiations.

Additionally, the parties need to discuss the question of exclusivity. Will the agreement be exclusive or non-exclusive? Can the licensor continue to use the patents and/or technology? Simply put, an exclusive license agreement is one in which the licensee is the only party who can use the patents and/or technology. A non-exclusive agreement means that the licensor can grant others the right to use the patents and/or technology. There is even a form of an exclusive agreement where the only other party who has the right to use the licensed property is the licensor. While it is almost certainly an advantage for the license to be exclusive from the licensee's perspective, the choice may simply not be an option. Certain licensors have set policies against the grant of exclusive licenses. If that is the case, the discussion concerning exclusivity will be quite short.

The Letter of Intent

One of the most effective ways to insure that oral negotiations between a licensor and a prospective licensee ultimately result in a formal license agreement is through the use of a simple letter of intent, which is entered into between the parties at the conclusion of their oral negotiations. The letter of intent is normally a one- or two-page letter from the licensor (generally prepared in advance by its attorney), which outlines the salient business considerations of the ultimate arrangement. When the attorney prepares the letter of intent, the specific business terms and conditions, such as the royalty rate, advance, territory, etc., are usually left blank. As such, the letter serves as the basis of the negotiations between the parties.

At the conclusion of the negotiations, the parties can then insert the appropriate numbers agreed upon during the negotiations. The letter of intent is intended to serve as a preliminary document to bind the parties for a limited period of time to particular terms and conditions. It is subject to a formal agreement being entered into within that period of time. The letter of intent should state that the failure to conclude a formal agreement by a predetermined date will result in expiration of the letter of intent.

Letters of intent are particularly useful when the initial negotiations are conducted by the licensing executives with the understanding that the matter will then be turned over to their respective attorneys for finalization of the formal agreement. Absent a letter of intent, it is often difficult to "conclude" negotiations. Business executives always seem to come up with new business issues to consider or to change (either on their own or with the "help" of their attorneys), and their attorneys unfailingly seem to raise so many legal issues that additional negotiations can drag on for days, if not months and years. The use of a letter of intent permits the business executives to conclude their active participation at an early date, usually at the conclusion of the oral negotiations. The letter of intent is then turned over to the respective attorneys for preparation of the final agreement.

Despite the existence of the letter of intent, parties will occasionally decide to reopen the negotiations. Nevertheless, once a deal has been struck and reduced to writing in the letter of intent, it is more likely that the executives will not try to renegotiate these agreed-to points. They begin to sell themselves (and others) on the idea that a license agreement has been struck, and they do not want to jeopardize that agreement.

Letters of intent are particularly effective in avoiding endless hassling between attorneys over legal (or even business) issues. As the letter of intent will generally include a time period within which a formal definitive agreement must be concluded, the attorneys are presented with an agreed-upon outline of the business terms and a deadline for the formal license agreement. If either side's attorney nit-picks over minor legal issues, he or she runs the risk of destroying the entire deal, which the client may consider a *fait accompli*. In negotiations, attorneys often need an impetus to proceed in an expeditious fashion and a deadline within which an agreement must be worked out. The letter of intent provides both.

Ideally, the letter of intent should address the following essential elements of the arrangement:

- the nature of the grant (exclusive v. non-exclusive);
- an identification of the property and product(s) to be covered by the license (e.g., patents, technology, etc.);
- the licensed territory;
- the term or period of the agreement;
- renewal options;
- the royalty rate, advances and guaranteed minimum royalties;
- the procedure for improvements to the original property;
- the party who will bear the responsibility for obtaining, maintaining and enforcing intellectual property rights;
- the date when manufacturing and distribution will commence;

- the amount of product liability insurance required; and
- the time period within which a definitive formal agreement will be worked out.

The Battle of Forms

When the parties conclude their initial round of negotiations, regardless of whether or not a letter of intent is signed, the time will come to memorialize their agreement in a formal, written license agreement. The first question that immediately comes to mind at this time is which party should take the responsibility for preparing the written agreement.

The answer to that question may depend on whether the license agreement is part of a large licensing program conducted by the licensor or is a one-shot agreement. In the first instance, the licensor will, undoubtedly, have a form agreement that it will present to the licensee for review and execution. The licensor's rationale in attempting to use such a form agreement is that it wants to standardize its licensing transactions, and that is understandable. The easiest way for a licensor to conduct a full-scale licensing program where many different licenses are granted is to use standard, form agreements so that the terms of one do not differ substantially from the terms of another. The licensor may have entered into a "favored nation" provision in an earlier agreement, which provides that it will not grant any future licenses on terms more favorable than the terms granted in that agreement. Consistency between agreements is one way to avoid such a problem.

Where the parties have little previous experience in licensing, the first order of business is to agree upon who will prepare the first draft of the agreement. It is the authors' strong belief that the party who prepares the first draft of the agreement has a decided advantage in the subsequent negotiations, since such a draft clearly positions the business deal most favorably to the drafting party. While there will clearly be some give and take between the parties before reaching the final version of the agreement, the party who prepares the first draft of the agreement is in the best position for the subsequent negotiations.

In most situations, the licensor will undertake the responsibility for preparing the first draft of the agreement. That is understandable since the licensor owns the intellectual property rights that will form the basis of the agreement. As such, the licensor has a vested interest in preserving the property rights. It should be appreciated that there is no such thing as a "standard" license agreement. Every agreement is different because every negotiation is different. A licensor-oriented license agreement may run thirty to forty pages in length and emphasize the obligations of the licensee. Conversely, a license agreement drafted by a licensee tends to be shorter and will emphasize the representations and warranties being made by the licensor.

Terminology

License agreements use somewhat unique terminology, and it is wise to clearly define all terms in the agreement to avoid any possible confusion. For example, most license agreements start with an identification of the parties, i.e., the property owner being referred to as the "licensor" and the party taking the license being referred to as the "licensee." One of the most important definitions in a license agreement is the definition of the "licensed property." If patents are involved, they may be referred to as the "licensed patents" and may (or may not) include pending applications. Similarly, if technology is involved, it may be referred to as the "licensed technology." *No matter what terms are used, it is imperative to clearly identify what these terms refer to.* Frequently, schedules of patents or technology are attached to the license agreement to more clearly define what the parties mean by the terms.

Similarly, the "licensed territory" is the area (typically geographical) in which the licensee may operate. Many patent and technology license agreements are restricted to the United States or North America, although worldwide agreements are not uncommon. The licensed territory will depend, in large measure, on the ability of the licensee to operate outside the United States as well as the scope of international patent protection obtained by the licensor. Presumably, the licensee cannot operate outside the licensed territory. The practical exception to that, however, is where the licensed territory is limited to a particular country, e.g., the United States, and the licensor has no patent protection in other countries. In such a situation, the licensee would be able to practice the invention on a royalty-free basis around the world even though it is subject to a royalty obligation in the licensed territory where the patents remain in force.

The effective period of the license agreement is referred to as the "term" of the agreement. The term of a typical patent and technology license agreement varies widely from one to several years. Even where the term of an agreement is short, the licensee may be granted one or more options to renew the agreement for additional "extended terms." Such options are typically subject to the licensee meeting certain minimal royalty obligations. For instance, the wording in an agreement might state: "The licensee is granted an option to renew this agreement for an additional five (5) year extended term provided that it has paid licensor earned royalties of at least $100,000 during the then in-effect term."

When the agreement includes a license under patents, licensors must be careful to avoid a situation where the term extends beyond the expiration of the last to expire patent. Requiring a licensee to continue to pay royalties beyond the expiration of a patent is a violation of the antitrust laws and is expressly prohibited. One way to minimize the impact of this prohibition when patents and technology are bundled together, is to assign separate royalty rates for each property form. Upon expiration of the patent, the licensee would be obligated to continue to pay the royalty for the technology portion of the agreement.

Grant of Rights

The grant of rights provision in a patent and technology license agreement is the heart and sole of the agreement. This is the provision in which the licensee is being granted the right to use the licensed property. This is the provision which will define the scope of the licensee's use of the licensed property, i.e., exclusive vs. non-exclusive. Frequently, the grant of rights provision will identify whether or not the licensee has the right to grant sublicenses to third parties and, if so, under what conditions.

Where the licensed property includes pending patent applications, the agreement should recite what happens in the event that the applications are finally rejected by the Patent and Trademark Office. A licensee will frequently agree to pay a licensor royalties for the opportunity to beat its competitor to the marketplace with a product that will be eventually patented. That same licensee, however, will probably be reluctant to continue paying the licensor for the right to market the same product that all of its competitors are able to market on a royalty-free basis.

Compensation

The manner in which the licensor is compensated for the use of the property by the licensee and any sublicensees can vary widely. Possible options include:

- a one-time lump sum payment to the licensor (sometimes called a "paid-up license");
- a set annual fee with no royalty;
- an ongoing royalty based solely on a percentage of licensee's sales of the licensed products with no advance or guaranteed minimum royalty payment;
- an ongoing royalty in a fixed amount based on each licensed product sold with no advance or guaranteed minimum royalty payment;
- an ongoing royalty based on a percentage of licensee's sales of the licensed products (or in a fixed amount based on each licensed product sold) with either or both an advance against royalties and an annual minimum royalty (which may or may not be guaranteed); or
- any combination of the above.

As the preceding demonstrates, the actual compensation package negotiated can take virtually any form and will vary from agreement to agreement. The most important requirement of the compensation provision, however, is that it fit the situation and meet the needs of the parties to the agreement.

We have left the calculation of typical royalties to the chapter on the valuation of intellectual property (Chapter Four). Generally speaking, however, the starting point for many royalty rate negotiations is five percent of the licensee's net sales of the licensed products. From that starting point, the actual negotiated royalty rate will rise or fall depending upon the circumstances of the transaction.

Most license agreements provide for the payment of an advance against royalties, typically due upon execution of the agreement. Advances range from several hundred dollars to millions, depending upon the transaction.

Some licensors require their licensees to pay guaranteed minimum royalties each year the agreements are in effect. In these situations, the licensee is obligated to achieve the minimum royalty figure for a particular period or run the risk of having the licensor terminate the agreement. Alternatively, the agreement could provide that the licensor does not have the right to terminate but may convert the agreement from an exclusive license agreement to a non-exclusive license. This gives the licensor the ability to grant similar non-exclusive licenses to third parties. The conversion of the agreement from exclusive to non-exclusive is a good approach for marginal properties that are capable of generating some revenue but not enough to warrant a large minimum royalty payment. Most agreements provide that the licensee may supplement its actual earned royalty payments to achieve the minimum royalty obligation. Thus, if the actual earned royalties fall behind the minimum royalty, the licensee may make an additional payment to meet such minimum royalty obligation and prevent the licensor from terminating the agreement or converting it to non-exclusive.

Guaranteed minimum royalty obligations are more onerous from the licensee's perspective since they require the licensee to supplement the earned royalty payments in the event that the earned royalties fail to achieve the minimum guarantee. While guaranteed minimum royalty provisions are quite common in merchandising agreements, they are far less common in patent and technology agreements.

Where the licensee intends to institute a sublicensing program around the property, the agreement should specify that the licensee has the right to grant sublicenses to third parties to manufacture different types of licensed products. It should further address how the licensor and the licensee will share any income derived from sublicensing. While most licensees agree that the licensor should share in revenues received from sublicensees, the question is to what extent? A fifty-fifty split between the licensor and the licensee of net sublicensing income is ostensibly fair, since it gives the licensee the ability to apply the costs of conducting the sublicensing program against such income prior to distribution. In such an arrangement, however, the parties will ultimately get into some sort of discussion as to what is and what is not an allocable expense. Was the ten-day trip the licensee's Vice-President took with his wife to Switzerland during the ski season really necessary even though he talked with two potential sublicensees?

A somewhat cleaner approach is to give the licensor a lower percentage but base the percentage on gross rather than net income. Each party would then be required to absorb his own expenses out of his own share of the income, and disputes as to allocable expenses would be avoided. A sixty-forty or even seventy-thirty split of gross income (without deduction of expenses) between the licensee and the licensor may therefore be easier to administer and will prevent any arguments between the parties. Moreover, such a split takes into account the differences in the contributions and responsibilities of the licensee and the licensor.

When the compensation provision requires the payment of a royalty, it is critical to define what the royalty will be paid on. In most agreements, the royalty will be calculated on "net sales" which is a defined term in the agreement. Frequently, net sales will be the gross sales of the licensed products less specific discounts, taxes and returns. The actual definition of net sales will, of course, vary from agreement to agreement and from industry to industry. Since the actual definition of net sales can significantly affect the royalty income due to a licensor, a licensor should pay close attention to what a licensee may and may not exclude from gross sales.

Accounting and Royalty Investigations

Where there is a royalty obligation on the part of the licensee, the licensor will want to include a provision giving it the right to conduct a royalty investigation or audit of the licensee's books and records. These books and records should not only include the licensee's sales records but also its manufacturing records to insure that there is some degree of correlation between the two. The purpose of such a provision is to insure that the licensee is paying its fair share of royalties.

Typically, the audit provision will give the licensor the right to inspect the licensee's books and records during the period of the license agreement. Some agreements require that the inspection only be conducted by a certified public accountant. This is particularly limiting, however, since most professional royalty investigators are not CPA's. For the licensee's protection, the provision will typically require that the licensor give proper notice before conducting a royalty investigation and limit the number of such investigations, for example, to no more than one per year.

The investigator representing the licensor should have the right to make copies of all relevant documents to support his or her claims, and the licensee should be required to fully cooperate with the licensor's investigator in this regard. Many licensees require that a confidentiality provision be included to protect their proprietary financial information.

It is quite common for the audit clause to include a provision that in the event that the investigation reveals an underpayment that is over a certain amount, the licensee will pay for the cost of the investigation. The predetermined amount is frequently a percentage of the total moneys properly due the licensor, for example, five percent. Attendant with the audit provision is a requirement that the licensee maintain its books and records for a minimum period of time, for example, for two to three years from the date to which they pertain. This protects the licensor from a situation where the licensee simply destroys its records to avoid an unfavorable report.

Improvements and Grant Backs

By its very nature, patent licensing involves cutting edge technology which is constantly changing. As such, it is quite common for improvements to be made to the technology during the term of the license agreement. Such improvements may be made by both the licensor and licensee. The license agreement should specifically address how such improvements will be handled and which party will ultimately own the rights to these improvements. If the licensor makes the improvements, the licensee will want to have them included in the license grant of the agreement, so that the licensee can benefit from these improvements. The improvements will, of course, be subject to the payment of a royalty. This insures that the licensee continues to have the latest and most up-to-date technology. It also prevents the licensor from licensing out the improvements to a licensee's competitor.

There are, however, situations where the licensee develops the improvement in the licensed technology. In such instances, the licensee should be the owner of the rights to such improvements and should be able to use those improvements on a royalty-free basis, provided that they are not subject to the superior rights of the licensor. In order to protect themselves from such situations, some licensors require that the licensee assign back to the licensor all rights in any improvements made during the term of the agreement. Such a provision is known as a "grant back" provision because the licensee is, in effect, granting back such rights to the licensor.

Understandably, most licensees do not favor such a provision and seek to have it stricken from most license agreements. While the inclusion of such a provision is seemingly against public policy, such provisions have, so far, managed to survive court challenges. See, for example, *Transparent Wrap Machine Corp. v. Stokes & Smith Co.*, 329 U.S. 637 (1947), where the Supreme Court held that assignment-type grant backs of patents representing improvements on the licensed patented inventions are not, per se, illegal. The court reasoned that the use of one legal monopoly to acquire another is proper.

Intellectual Property Responsibilities

Who has the obligation to obtain and maintain patent rights? What about foreign patent protection? Which party has the right to sue infringers, and who pays for such a suit? If there is a recovery against an infringer, who gets to retain any recovery? These are questions that constantly arise in the context of a licensing arrangement and should be specifically addressed in the license agreement.

Generally speaking, the licensor has the responsibility to obtain and maintain intellectual property rights. Considering the fact that it is the licensor's patent rights that are involved and the licensee is paying for the ability to use such rights, that is only fair. A property owner should think long and hard before allowing another to take the responsibility to protect its intellectual property.

The question of foreign patents is not as clear, however. As indicated earlier, foreign patent protection must be acquired on a country-by-country basis and, as such, is quite expensive. Accordingly, many property owners (particularly the smaller ones) are simply not in a financial position to undertake a foreign filing program without some assistance from their licensees. In such instances, it is not uncommon for the licensee to advance the costs associated with a foreign filing program to the licensor with the understanding that it will be able to take a credit against its royalty obligations in the amount of such expenses. This benefits both parties.

The right to sue infringers typically vests with the licensor. Most of the intellectual property statutes provide that actions can only be brought by the owner of the intellectual property rights. Some courts have, however, held that an exclusive licensee can bring an action for infringement. However, many license agreements provide that an infringement action can only be brought by the licensor. In those situations where the licensor fails to commence an action within a predefined period of time, for example, three months from the date of notification by the licensee, the licensee may be permitted to commence an action of its own. In such event, the licensee may have the right to join the licensor in the action if necessary.

Typically, the party bringing the lawsuit has the responsibility for paying its costs. In most cases, that party will also have the right to retain any moneys recovered from an infringer. There are instances, however, where the parties will agree to share, according to some formula, any recovery after the repayment of any costs and expenses in bringing the action. It is important that the agreement address this issue, regardless of the way in which it is finally resolved. A licensor's failure to address this issue has given at least one licensee the opportunity to allege that it was entitled a percentage of recoveries from an infringement action, since it was damaged by the infringing sales.

"Favored Nations" Clauses

Many licensees will want some assurance from the licensor that they have received the best deal possible. They want protection against a licensor going out and giving their competitor a more favorable arrangement. When seeking such an assurance, a licensee may request what is called a "favored nations" clause. Such a clause will typically provide that the licensor shall not subsequently enter into agreements for the same property on terms more favorable than those given to the licensee. In the event that the licensor does, in fact, grant a more favorable license, the licensee would either have the right to terminate the agreement or, alternatively, have the agreement modified to include the more favorable provisions. This is clearly a licensee-oriented provision which many licensors adamantly refuse to include in any agreement. As can be appreciated, its implications are endless since it can easily affect virtually every license agreement granted by the licensor.

Representations, Warranties and Indemnification

Every licensor must be prepared to make certain representations and warranties relative to the licensed property. That is, after all, the reason the licensee is agreeing to pay the licensor a royalty. Most licensors should be prepared to provide their licensees with the following assurances:

- they own the underlying intellectual property rights;
- they have not granted any rights to any other

party in conflict with the rights being conveyed in the agreement; and
- use of the licensed property by the licensee will not infringe upon the rights of any third party.

These representations and warranties are relatively standard in the licensing industry, and licensees should insist on their inclusion in the license agreement. Smaller licensors may ask to limit their representations concerning non-infringement to the assurance that the property will not infringe on third parties to "the best of their knowledge and belief" to protect themselves against potentially superior rights of which they are unaware. That is fair. Similarly, most licensees should be prepared to warrant that they will use their best efforts to promote and sell the licensed products. It is not uncommon for such a warranty to be negotiated down to "reasonable commercial efforts" which is, obviously, a much lower standard.

Both licensors and licensees should be prepared to indemnify the other for any breaches of the agreement's representations and warranties. For example, should another party sue the licensee for infringement of a patent, the licensor should be prepared to defend and indemnify the licensee with respect to such action.

Termination

The termination provision of any license agreement is perhaps the most important provision in the agreement, particularly from the perspective of the licensor. Assuming that licensing arrangements always work the way both parties expected them to when they signed the original agreements, there would be no need to ever again review the license agreement. Unfortunately, agreements do not always work out as planned. When problems develop, the first provision reviewed in any license agreement is the termination provision. Surprisingly, in many license agreements, this provision is inadequate or totally absent. The termination provision safeguards the licensor from making a licensing mistake that could be devastating to the entire licensing program. If the licensee does not perform to the expected standards set forth in the agreement, the licensor can terminate the agreement and start again with a new licensee.

The licensor should be in a position to terminate the agreement immediately if the licensee does not introduce the product on or before the product introduction date recited in the license agreement or does not begin shipping product on or before the first shipment date. Licensors should hold fast to the inclusion of such dates to insure that the licensee is, in fact, serious about the license. Licensors should also be in a position to immediately terminate the agreement upon the occurrence of certain dire events, most notably:

- the repeated failure of the licensee to make payments when due (two or more times during any calendar year);
- a recall of the licensed products by a governmental agency;
- the failure of the licensee to maintain required insurance coverage; or
- the failure of the licensee to continuously sell the licensed product.

In addition to the above, each party should have

the right to terminate the agreement on notice (normally thirty days) in the event of a breach of a material provision of the agreement by the other party and the failure to cure that breach within the notice period. The license agreement should contain a "post termination rights" provision which, among other things, requires that the licensee submit an inventory of all product on hand at the time of termination and provides for a sell-off period by the licensee of such inventory for a limited time subject to the payment of royalties.

Governing Law and Disputes

Standard boilerplate provisions also provide for what law will govern in a dispute between the parties and more importantly, how and where the dispute will be resolved. In domestic licensing situations, the governing law is of less importance since federal law will typically apply. It can, however, become more problematic in international licensing situations.

How and where disputes will be resolved is a more important consideration. The choice is typically litigation versus arbitration. While attorneys differ with respect to the pros and cons of each (typically influenced by their prior experiences), in international transactions arbitration does offer many advantages, particularly where one party does not have a presence in the United States. If arbitration is chosen, the parties should make sure that the wording of the arbitration provision is sufficient to confer jurisdiction. The American Arbitration Association makes available a sample arbitration provision that is readily accepted by virtually all courts.

Upon deciding the manner in which disputes will

be resolved, the parties should also decide where the proceeding will be held. If arbitration is the vehicle of choice, the parties should agree where the arbitration will be held and under what rules. A sample provision which addresses this concern is the following: "The arbitration will be conducted before a single arbitrator in accordance with the then in-effect rules of the American Arbitration Association at its New York City office." The parties may also want to reach an agreement upon what, if any, portion of an arbitrator's award can be appealed and to where such appeal can be made.

Alternatively, if litigation is the dispute resolution vehicle of choice, the parties should agree which court will hear such action and then state that the parties consent to the jurisdiction of such court. The parties may even want to agree among themselves to limit the typical types of defenses otherwise available to them, e.g., lack of jurisdiction, improper venue, etc.

Assignability and Sublicensing

Most licensors do not want their licensees to have the ability to assign their license agreements to another party without the prior express written consent of the licensor. Licensors are afraid that the licensee may assign the agreement to a direct competitor of the licensor or, alternatively, to a party that is financially unable to meet the obligations of the agreement. As such, licensors will frequently include a provision in the agreement restricting the right of the licensee to assign the agreement.

Similarly, some licensors are reluctant to permit the licensee to enter into sublicense agreements, particularly where it might reduce the income they receive. It should be appreciated that there is a difference between sublicensing and the right to manufacture. Many licensees contract with off-shore companies to manufacture licensed products for them. That is not sublicensing and is typically permitted under an agreement. Sublicensing involves a situation where the sublicensee literally steps into the shoes of the licensee and assumes all of the benefits (and obligations) of the license agreement. Such arrangements typically require the prior express written approval of the licensor.

Integration

Last, but not least, the agreement should include an integration clause which provides that the license agreement is the final and entire understanding between the parties, incorporates all prior written or oral agreements between the parties and may not be changed or modified except by written agreement signed by all parties. The purpose of this provision is to limit one party's ability to rely on a prior oral representation.

Seven: Antitrust Considerations

All license agreements, strategic alliances and joint ventures involving intellectual property involve antitrust issues. Similarly, all licenses involving patents and copyrights should take into account patent or copyright misuse issues. While related, antitrust and patent misuse analyses are distinct in both definition and enforcement. Under any circumstance, all the parties to a technology license agreement must consider the potential impact the license will have on the marketplace and the potential antitrust consequences thereof. If necessary, the parties should seek the opinion of counsel with respect to this extremely specialized area of the law.

The Basics of U.S. Antitrust Law

All technology licenses in the U.S. are, in effect, subject to the constraints and prohibitions of the antitrust laws and their implementing regulations. All antitrust scrutiny begins with Sections 1 and 2 of the Sherman Act. Section 1 of the Sherman Act expressly prohibits conspiracies, contracts and other combinations, between at least two participants not under common control, that place an unreasonable restraint on trade. There are two standards for such an assessment, a "per se" standard and a "rule of reason." If a court determines that the restraint at issue, such as price-fixing, is "per se" illegal, the practice at issue will be conclusively ruled harmful and illegal, and there will be no inquiry into the specific harm caused by the practice, nor into the justification for such practice. In effect, the practice is illegal regardless of its effect on the marketplace. Most sales or market-related restraints of trade among competitors (so-called "horizontal" conduct) will generally be judged to be per se illegal. If the practice at issue does not satisfy the "per se" standard, it will be judged by the "rule of reason," standard, which will include inquiries into the purpose and impact of the practice, as well as potential justifications therefore. According to this standard, the practice may or may not be illegal, depending on the its effects on the marketplace.

Section 2 of the Sherman Act primarily regulates willful monopolies and/or conspiracies to monopolize. Violations of theses two sections may lead to both civil and criminal penalties, with many per se illegal activities (such as price fixing) resulting in criminal prosecution by the U.S. Department of Justice.

Other antitrust laws of particular interest for technology licensors are Section 5 of the Federal Trade Commission (FTC) Act, which prohibits "unfair methods of competition," and Sections 3 and 7 of the Clayton Act, which prohibit exclusive contracts, tie-ins or mergers and acquisitions which lessen competition or create monopolies. Assignments and exclusive licenses of patents, copyrights and trademarks are considered to be asset acquisitions, and therefore subject to Section 7 of the Clayton Act. Significantly, with the exception of the FTC Act provisions, which are enforceable only by the FTC, all of these statutes (including the Sherman Act) may be enforced by the

FTC, Department of Justice, State Attorneys General or private litigants.

Antitrust issues under Section 7 of the Clayton Act would likely be raised when a party which has market power in a particular market acquires, through a joint venture or an exclusive license, a patent license in its market. *See, e.g., SCM Corp. v. Xerox Corp.,* 645 F.2d 1195 (2d Cir. 1981), *cert. denied,* 455 U.S. 1016 (1982)). Similarly, the practice of requiring "tie-ins" — where a purchaser of one product is required to purchase another product from that same seller as a condition of the sale — may be found to be a per se illegal violation of Section 1 of the Sherman Act if market power over the tying product can be shown. *See, e.g., Eastman Kodak Co. v. Image Technical Services, Inc.,* 112 S.Ct. 2072 (1992).

Antitrust considerations must also be considered when pursuing joint ventures, particularly where such arrangements are made between competitors. Joint ventures between competitors which are limited to research and development are encouraged by certain federal regulations and will be given a "rule of reason" analysis. However, those which deal more closely with a combination of the parties' respective operations will be given more strict scrutiny. In such situations, it is important to structure the joint venture in such a way as to restrict access to confidential business information not immediately necessary to the success of the venture. Specifically, the parties should be careful to restrict the venture from overlapping into other areas of the business, particularly areas which affect pricing, so as to avoid the appearance that the cooperation between the parties will somehow result in a scheme to fix prices. Joint venture partners would also be wise to implement an educational program for their respective employees in order to remind them that there are antitrust consequences of the venture and as a means to reinforce what conduct is important for them to avoid.

The Microsoft Example

Those previously unfamiliar with the government's interest in monitoring the antitrust aspects of intellectual property transactions could not have missed all of the publicity surrounding the consent decree negotiated between the U.S. Department of Justice and the Microsoft Corporation, after over four years of investigation by the government. Since 1991, the DOJ and FTC had been investigating long-standing complaints by Microsoft's rivals that Microsoft had used its licensing clout to dominate the software business in violation of federal antitrust statutes. Specifically, the DOJ accused Microsoft of the following illegal practices:

- requiring manufacturers interested in Microsoft's MS-DOS operating system to purchase other Microsoft products (an improper "tie-in" as defined above).
- administering exclusionary "per processor" licenses (requiring the payment of a royalty for each machine manufactured whether or not the licensed software was installed in the machine) and licenses which obligated licensees to purchase Microsoft products beyond the lifetime of the master operating system (an alleged attempt to prohibit the development of a competing system); and

- using overly restrictive nondisclosure agreements in an effort to restrict the abilities of some licensees to work with developers of competing operating systems.

On July 15, 1994, a proposed consent decree between the DOJ and Microsoft was filed with the U.S. District Court for the District of Columbia. By virtue of this decree, Microsoft agreed to refrain from certain licensing practices for a term of six and one-half years in order to settle the government's accusations. Specifically, the decree prohibits Microsoft from:

- entering into "per processor" licenses;
- requiring computer manufacturers to purchase minimum numbers of Microsoft operating systems;
- utilizing license terms of over one year (renewal provisions notwithstanding);
- requiring payment on a "lump sum" basis;
- requiring the purchase (or license) of other Microsoft software products as a condition of obtaining a license to a Microsoft operating system; and
- incorporating restrictive nondisclosure agreements in licenses with potential software developers.

As a footnote, the settlement was initially rejected by the presiding U.S. District Court judge on the grounds that it did not go far enough in restricting Microsoft's alleged attempts to restrict competition. However, joint appeals by Microsoft and the Department of Justice to the Court of Appeals ultimately resulted in approval of the consent decree.

The New Antitrust Guidelines

On April 6, 1995, the Department of Justice (DOJ) and the Federal Trade Commission (FTC) issued its long-awaited revised Antitrust Guidelines for Intellectual Property Licensing. Like all regulations, these regulations are not a foolproof "roadmap" for avoiding antitrust pitfalls in technology licensing, nor are they free from ambiguities. They do, however, codify some of the government's positions as to how it views intellectual property licenses (generally considered to be pro-competitive), and how it will scrutinize the antitrust considerations of said licenses.

Included in the regulations are guidelines for mergers and asset acquisitions. As noted above, because exclusive licenses are treated as "acquisitions" for antitrust purposes, the effect of an acquisition by a party which already possesses market power in the particular area will be scrutinized. According to the Guidelines, such a transaction will not be considered problematic unless it results in one party obtaining a market share which exceeds twenty percent. High level acquisitions and/or mergers, including exclusive patent licenses, involving large sums of money ($15 million for acquisitions and $10 million for joint ventures) will still require a special filing with the federal government (a so-called Hart-Scott-Rodino filing), as well as the payment of a significant fee.

The DOJ Guidelines also address the practice of "tie-ins." As noted above, the Supreme Court, in the *Eastman Kodak* case, maintained that tie-ins may be a per se illegal violation of Section 1 of the Sherman Act if market power over the tying product can be established. The Guidelines, however, indicate that tie-ins will be scrutinized under a "rule of reason" approach even when the licensor requiring the tie-in has market power. This is an attempt by the government to balance the alleged anti-competitive effects of tie-in practices with their alleged efficiencies. Because the two approaches represent differing views, any party considering a tie-in as a condition to a license agreement would be wise to give its licensee a legitimate alternative to the tie-in arrangement, regardless of its market power.

The DOJ Guidelines also address the practice of restricting the licensed territory or field of use, both of which are significant in negotiating technology license agreements involving patents or copyrights. These practices are generally considered to be "vertical" restraints, and, as such, are presumptively permissible under the Guidelines, provided that the license is valid and intended to result in increased business efficiency. The Guidelines recognize that such restrictions are within the inherent scope of a patent or copyright grant. The Guidelines also provide that vertical restraints may exist in licenses between parties whose market shares are below twenty percent of the affected market. It should be noted, however, that so-called post-sale vertical restraints (attempts by the licensor to control the licensee's subsequent activities) are evaluated under the "rule of reason" analysis with the exception of price restraints, which remain per se illegal. Although there may be some *extremely limited* circumstances where a post-sale price restriction in a patent license may be permitted (*See, e.g., United States v. General Electric*, 272 U.S. 476 (1976)), strong language in the DOJ Guidelines against any such practices make it wise to avoid price restrictions in technology licenses.

Patent Misuse and Technology Licensing

Patent misuse is a doctrine that is often mistakenly confused with antitrust prohibitions. Unlike antitrust doctrines, which are derived from specific governmental laws and regulations, patent misuse is a judicially-created affirmative defense intended to prevent a patentee from abusing the exclusivity granted by an issued patent.

Patent misuse as an equitable defense to a charge of patent infringement was first developed by the United States Supreme Court in *Morton Salt Co. v. G.S. Suppinger Co.*, 314 U.S. 488 (1942). In response to a charge of infringement of the plaintiff's patent for a particular machine, the Supreme Court held that the plaintiff's attempts to require patent licensees to purchase non-patented products from the plaintiff for use with the patented machine was an attempt to use its patent in a manner contrary to public policy. Thus, the Supreme Court ruled that this "misuse" rendered the patent unenforceable until such time that the specific misuse and any substantial lasting effects were purged.

Another form of patent misuse, and one that has potentially greater impact on technology licensing, was articulated by the Supreme Court in *Brulotte v. Thys Co.*, 379 U.S. 29 (1964). In this case, the Supreme Court held that a patent license agreement which extended royalty payments beyond the life of the subject patent was an unlawful attempt to extend the patent monopoly and a *per se* example of patent misuse.

It should be noted that Congress has, on several occasions, considered legislation that would eliminate or modify the per se application of the doctrine of patent misuse. Ultimately, however, the only modifications were codified in 35 U.S.C. Sec. 271(d) by adding a provision that a refusal to license is not patent misuse (35 U.S.C. 271(d)(4)), and a provision that product tying does not constitute patent misuse unless the licensor "has market power in the relevant market for the patent or patented product on which the license or sale is conditioned" (35 U.S.C. 271(d)(5)).

In the case of *Lasercomb America, Inc. v. Reynolds*, 911 F.2d 970 (4th Cir. 1990), the misuse doctrine was extended to copyrights by the Court of Appeals of the Fourth Circuit. In this case, as an affirmative defense to a charge of copyright infringement, the defendant asserted that the plaintiff's attempts to restrict the software development programs of its licensees violated public policy. In particular, the defendant charged that the language in the plaintiff's software license agreements requiring the licensee to refrain from developing any kind of similar software for 99 years, was a misuse of the plaintiff's copyright rights in its licensed software. The Fourth Circuit agreed, further holding that the defendant had the right to assert the claim of copyright misuse even though the defendant had not entered into a license with the plaintiff. In finding that the defendant did not have to show direct injury by the offending restrictions, the Fourth Circuit held that the defendant was only required to show that at least one other licensee had entered into a license agreement that contained the offensive language in order for the defendant to have standing to raise copyright misuse as an affirmative defense to a charge of infringement.

What is the impact of the misuse doctrine on the average license agreement? Most importantly, patent licensors may not use the license agreement to extend royalty payments beyond the life of the licensed patent. For this reason, many licensors will insist on a paid-up license in lieu of a running royalty. Others will refrain from granting a license solely based on patents and instead will insist that the license grant include the technology and know-how behind the patent, and, if appropriate, any trademarks associated therewith. In such cases, the license should specifically apportion a percentage of the earned royalty to each of the individual components of the license grant. The license should expressly note that upon expiration of the licensed patent, the total royalty will be reduced by the percentage specifically allocated to the patent, but that the licensee will be obligated to pay the remainder for its use of the technology and/or trademarks for the duration of the term of the agreement. While there is no "magic formula" that will preclude all claims of patent misuse, it is generally recommended that the percentage of the total royalty directed to the patent be between one-third and one-half of the total amount, unless there are special circumstances that can specifically justify a lesser amount. From the standpoint of the licensor, who obviously wants its total royalty to decrease as little as possible, the larger decrease will go further in removing any potential claim of patent misuse.

With respect to copyright misuse, the lesson taught by the *Lasercomb* case relates to the restrictions that a licensor of software many place on the actions of the licensee. Clearly, in *Lasercomb*, the court was highly offended by the licensor's attempt to use the license agreement to restrict its licensee's activities for 99 years following the term of the license. As in the case of most restrictive covenants, courts will probably strictly examine any such restrictions and are likely to construe them against the licensor, especially if the licensor and/or the licensed product occupies a dominant position in the marketplace. Thus, any attempt to utilize a license to restrict the business activities of the licensee, especially after the expiration of the agreement, is a risky practice indeed.

Eight:
International Licensing

As we approach the twenty-first century, it is clear that we are truly, for the first time, experiencing the age of the "global economy." New emerging markets are everywhere. The breakup of the Soviet Union and the former Eastern block nations has created new markets craving western technology. For the first time, there is now the opportunity for western companies to gain access to previously secret Soviet aerospace technology. The easement of trade and market restrictions in the People's Republic of China has also encouraged the influx of foreign investment and technology. In the Pacific Rim, South Korea has adopted a crash industrial agenda program in an attempt to supplant Japan as the premier developer of high technology in the region. The diffusion of military tensions in the Middle East has allowed more energy and resources to be spent developing a technology base. Clearly, there are new markets opening on an almost weekly basis.

Foreign Export Controls

All licensors who hope to exploit their technology overseas must first understand that all transfers of technical data from the United States to foreign entities are managed by federal export controls. The failure to comply with regulatory requirements can result in the loss of patent rights and the imposition of civil and criminal penalties.

Technology transfer licenses involving generally commercial uses, including commodities, technology and software (excepting those technologies specifically controlled by other agencies), will be subject to the control of the Department of Commerce's Bureau of Export Administration through the Export Administration Act of 1979 ("EAA"), 50 U.S.C. Sec. 2402 et seq. This agency has promulgated a list of categories of controlled technologies as well as a list of sub-categories, such as equipment, software, and/or technical data, for each category. Under these regulations, one of three types of licenses are needed for either the export or release of technical data, further depending upon the destination of the technology (some jurisdictions are given priority). It is the responsibility of the licensor to investigate the Bureau's current regulations and to make certain that it has the proper export license.

The first license available from the Bureau of Export Administration is a general license, which is granted for "publicly available" data, to all destinations. The second license, available for most non-nuclear technologies, is designed to prohibit the export of certain technologies to certain territories. Although a formal license from the Bureau is not required, the licensor should require written assurance from the transferee that the data will not be shipped into a prohibited territory before the product or technology is exported. With respect to all technical data which cannot be exported under the first two licenses, the licensor will be required to obtain a so-called "validated license," which requires a formal license application and supporting letter form the licensor.

The State Department's Office of Defense Trade Controls ("ODTC") controls the export of defense articles and related technical data, including munitions, certain military software and many space-related items. Exporters of such items must register before the ODTC and obtain the requisite license. With respect to nuclear technology, the Department of Energy has established regulations relating to the export of nuclear-related technical data, and has established a schedule of activities which are generally authorized. If the technology is nuclear-related and does not fall within the schedule, specific authorization will be required.

Finally, the licensor should be aware that the Invention Secrecy Act of 1951, (35 U.S.C. Secs. 181 et seq.) provides that inventors shall not file a patent application in a foreign country based upon an "invention made in this country" until six months after the filing of a U.S. patent application, unless a foreign filing license is granted by the U.S. Patent Office. Further to this Act, all patent applications are given a preliminary review by the Patent Office for material that may be related to national security. Most applications are cleared quickly, and the foreign filing license will usually be issued with the formal filing receipt (approximately three months from the date of filing). The foreign filing license will also cover all modifications, supplements and amendments to the initial patent application. Those applications which may relate to national security will be forwarded to the appropriate defense agency for further scrutiny by the Patent Office for a national security inspection, which will take approximately six months. If it is determined that the application contains material which may relate to national security, the Patent Office may request issuance of a secrecy order requiring the applicant to maintain the invention in secret. The secrecy order may also set forth the applicable export controls for the technical data contained in the application, and may also identify those countries where a patent application may be filed. Other secrecy orders may, however, be more restrictive, depending upon the technology involved. Patent applicants must understand that while some applications under secrecy orders (excepting those which involve atomic energy and nuclear inventions) may be filed in certain foreign countries due to the presence of defense treaties, the violation of the Patent Office rules concerning secrecy can be severe. Unless the applicant is able to obtain a retroactive license (based upon error without deceptive intent), the applicant may be subject to civil and criminal penalties as well as suffer the loss of its patent rights.

All license agreements involving the transfer of technology overseas should take into account the possible need for governmental approval. The agreement should also protect the licensor from having to divulge technical data until the necessary licenses have been obtained, as well as indicate that the licensor will take appropriate steps to secure the requisite export licenses.

The following is a sample of the language that should be included in any international license agreement regarding government approval:

U.S. GOVERNMENTAL APPROVAL

(a) Promptly after the execution of this Agreement, and at LICENSOR's expense, LICENSOR shall take all necessary and reasonable

steps to obtain all required export licenses from the appropriate governmental agencies.
(b) Upon LICENSOR's request, and at the expense of LICENSOR, LICENSEE shall provide LICENSOR, in a timely manner, all information required by LICENSOR or by a governmental agency in furtherance of LICENSOR's efforts to obtain the requisite export licenses.
(c) LICENSOR shall not be required to disclose to LICENSEE or otherwise export to LICENSEE any licensed technology, data, know-how and/or licensed products until such time as all necessary governmental approvals and/or export licenses have been granted.
(d) In the event that any licensed technology, data, know-how and/or licensed products is in any way subject to a secrecy order or similar restriction, LICENSOR shall take all reasonable steps to seek permits, modifications and/or rescissions of such secrecy order in furtherance of this Agreement. However, until such permits, modifications and/or rescissions have been granted, LICENSOR shall not be required to disclose to LICENSEE or otherwise export to LICENSEE any licensed technology, data, know-how and/or licensed products subject to said secrecy order.

Protection of Intellectual Property and Trade Secrets

The cornerstone of technology licensing is the proprietary nature of the licensed technology. Much of its inherent value is directly related to its secrecy. Companies spend considerable time and assets in protecting their technologies through patents and trade secret programs.

It is perhaps axiomatic that there will be considerable loss in the inherent value of licensed technology if the proprietary nature of same is compromised. As discussed previously, developing a patent portfolio in countries outside of the United States can be quite expensive. Even if one were to have the resources to obtain patents overseas, there are many countries throughout the world which do not have a history of supporting the proprietary rights of foreigners. Some nations, such as Taiwan, seek to preserve an advantage for its nationals by making it difficult, if not impossible, for a foreign entity to obtain a valid patent. Others, such as China and India, have a poor record of enforcing the rights of intellectual property owners against third party infringers. In addition, some of the nations which emerged from the former Soviet block are still in the process of developing viable patent registration and judicial systems.

Is it simply a situation of licensing at one's own risk? Not entirely. There are certain precautions that the prudent licensor may take. The first (which also holds true in domestic situations) would be to find out as much about the potential licensee as is possible. The licensor should try to develop a strong sense of the licensee's business reputation in both its native country and with those foreign companies with whom it does business. If necessary, the licensor should enlist the services of an investigator in the licensee's host country.

It is also prudent that the prospective licensee be required to sign agreements relating to the confidentiality of all materials disclosed. In this regard, it is advisable to seek advice from local counsel to be certain that such language will conform to local standards and will allow for the greatest degree of enforcement available in the licensee's country.

The following is a sample of the language that should be included in any international license agreement regarding confidentiality:

CONFIDENTIALITY

> (a) LICENSEE shall take all reasonable steps to safeguard the Property from any unauthorized use, duplication, sublicensing or distribution.
>
> (b) It is recognized that during the course of its work with LICENSOR, LICENSEE may have occasion to conceive, create, develop, review or receive information which is considered by LICENSOR to be confidential or proprietary, including information relating to the Property, including inventions, patent, trademark and copyright applications, improvements, know-how, specifications, drawings, cost data, process flow diagrams, customer and supplier lists, bills, ideas and/or any other written material referring to same (the "Confidential Information"). Both during the Term of this Agreement and thereafter, LICENSEE agrees to maintain in confidence

such Confidential Information unless or until:

(i) it shall have been made public by an act or omission of a party other than itself;

(ii) LICENSEE receives such Confidential Information from an unrelated third party on a non-confidential basis; or

(iii) the passage of ten (10) years from the date of the disclosure of such Confidential Information to LICENSEE, whichever shall first occur.

(c) LICENSEE further agrees to use all reasonable precautions to assure that all such Confidential Information is properly protected and kept from unauthorized persons or disclosure.

(d) If requested by LICENSOR, LICENSEE agrees to promptly return to LICENSOR all materials, writings, equipment, models, mechanisms and the like obtained from or through LICENSOR including, but not limited to, all Confidential Information, all of which LICENSEE recognizes is the sole and exclusive property of LICENSOR.

(e) LICENSEE agrees that it will not, without first obtaining the prior written permission of LICENSOR:

(i) directly or indirectly utilize such Confidential Information in its own business; or

(ii) manufacture and/or sell any product which is based in whole or in part on such Confidential Information; or

(iii) disclose such Confidential Information to any third party.

Language such as the above should be used in addition to the standard language prohibiting the licensee from claiming any rights in the licensed technology.

Local Regulations

In some foreign countries, all licenses between resident companies and overseas entities must be registered with the host government, primarily as means of exercising control over the overseas remittance of hard currency. In some countries, such registration is limited to patent and technology agreements, while others require intellectual property licenses, including those involving trademarks and copyrights, to be recorded as a prerequisite for the remittance of royalties. Recordation requirements usually govern license transactions involving related companies, as well as those between companies at arm's length.

Recordation requirements are found in many Pacific Rim nations as well as in South America. Brazil, for example, requires that all intellectual property licenses be recorded in the Brazilian Patent and Trademark Office as a prerequisite for the remittance of royalties. However, in response to governmental directives intended to liberalize the economy and encourage foreign investment, certain restrictions have been relaxed. As of February 9, 1993, certain recordation requirements between related companies have been relaxed, although recordation is still required as a prerequisite for enforcement of the agreement against third parties, for the remittance of royalties and for certain taxation advantages. Furthermore, although the examination of license agreements by the Brazilian authorities will be restricted to a checking of the validity of the patents and trademark registrations licensed therein, it should be noted that it is still necessary to record all license agreements between unrelated companies.

In addition to seeking the assistance of local counsel in complying with local recordation requirements, it is also advisable to request assurance from the foreign entity itself that it will take all necessary steps to comply with local laws. The following is a sample of the language that should be included in any international license agreement with respect to compliance with local laws:

> COMPLIANCE WITH LOCAL LAWS
>
> (a) LICENSEE shall assure compliance with all applicable laws and regulations in each country in the Territory.
> (b) LICENSEE shall cooperate promptly with LICENSOR to assist LICENSOR in complying with all U.S. laws and laws of the each country in the Territory.

Currency

Clearly, the purpose of licensing one's technology is the expectation of profit from the licensee's use of same. While it is possible to structure a license whereby the licensor receives his profit through a technology exchange or in the form of a joint venture, most licensors wish to receive that most tangible form of profit — money. Some foreign governments make it extremely difficult to transfer hard currency out of the country. There may be heavy taxes imposed, as well as cumbersome governmental reporting regulations. This is another situation where the prospective licensor should seek the assistance of experienced local counsel, who can help navigate the licensor through the regulatory mine field.

In some countries, such as the new republics formed out of the dissolved Soviet Union nations, the issue is more basic. Simply put, there is not a lot of currency available to finance the acquisition of foreign technology. Potential licensors will, therefore, have to come up with more creative arrangements in order to reap the benefits of the licensed technology. Such arrangements would generally be in the form of joint ventures, barter arrangements and technology buybacks. In short, there is a desperate need to come up with means of compensation that does not involve the exchange of hard currency.

In order to protect itself from burdensome changes in foreign laws which may affect the transfer of earned royalties to the licensor, many technology licensors will eschew royalties altogether in favor of a paid-up license. This will prevent the licensor from having to chase the licensee for money at a later point and will avoid problems that result from changes in currency transfer regulations. Where this is not possible, however, it is imperative that licensors include provisions in the license agreement to protect their ability to receive royalties. A sample of such language is as follows:

CURRENCY

(a) All payments due LICENSOR shall be made in United States currency (converted from any foreign currency at the spot rate of exchange for United States Dollars as published by *The Wall Street Journal* in New York, NY, USA) by check drawn on a United States bank, unless otherwise specified by LICENSOR.

(b) All payments due LICENSOR based upon sales in countries outside of the United States shall accrue in the currency of the country in which the sales are made. LICENSEE shall utilize its best efforts to effect United States dollar transfers with respect to all such payments. However, any and all loss of exchange value, taxes or other expenses incurred in the transfer or conversion of foreign currency into United States dollars, and any income, remittance, or other taxes on such payments required to be withheld at the source shall be the exclusive responsibility of LICENSOR. In the event that LICENSEE is prevented by the laws and regulations of any country from transmitting all or any part of any payment due hereunder in United States dollars, LICENSEE shall transfer payment in such other currency as LICENSOR may request.

(c) In the event that currency regulations of a country in the Territory prohibit the payment of monies to LICENSOR or its nominee, LICENSEE shall deposit in LICENSOR's name in an account in the country designated by LICENSOR the amount due and furnish LICENSOR with proof of deposit. Such deposit shall satisfy LICENSEE's obligations hereunder with respect to such monies for so long as such restrictions prevail.

Licensing in the European Community

Clearly, the developed economies and the strong technology base of the European nations make them tremendously attractive markets in which to license technology. However, different intellectual property laws as well as the laws and regulations of the European Economic Community (EEC) present unique challenges to licensors structuring agreements. Many of the EEC regulations were designed to promote the free flow of goods and services among member states. However, these regulations often conflict with the desire of a patentee to carefully restrict the manufacture and use of the patented item to a particular territory or market. As such, parties to an international license agreement must consider the antitrust aspects of the transaction as defined under the laws of the EEC.

Trade among EEC member nations is governed by the Treaty of Rome, which was implemented to remove barriers to the free flow of goods and services across national boundaries. Primarily relevant to licensing situations are Articles 30, 36, 85 and 86 of the Treaty. Articles 30 and 36 concern the free movement of goods between member states, while Articles 85 and 86 reflect the basic rules concerning competition.

Specifically, Article 85(1) prohibits agreements which "may affect trade between Member States and which have as their object of effect the prevention, restriction or distortion of competition within the common context." This has been interpreted to prohibit such practices as price fixing. Article 86 prohibits "Abuse ... of a dominant position within the common market or in a substantial part of it ... as may affect trade between Member States." Practices specifically prohibited under Article 86 by definition include "limiting production, markets or technical developments," among others. This would appear to place a significant restriction on the ability of a licensor to exploit its technology, as a breakthrough technological development can readily result in its producer acquiring a "dominant position" in the marketplace, which, under EEC regulations, would generally be considered to be more than forty percent of the relevant market.

This does not mean that license agreements are prohibited under the Treaty of Rome. While the European Court of Justice may investigate situations which may be in violation of Articles 85 and 86, the parties to the agreement may apply for an exemption pursuant to Article 85(3). Article 85(3) specifically allows for an exemption for certain practices, if the agreement or practice in question "contributes to improving the production or distribution of goods or to promoting technological or economic progress, while allowing consumers a fair share of the resulting benefit." In addition, the EEC has issued Block Exemption Regulations, which set forth specific license restrictions which may be automatically exempt from Article 85(1) of the Treaty of Rome.

The block exemption regulations apply to both patent and know-how licenses and to combined patent and know-how licenses. The best way for the licensor to understand the block exemptions is to remember that they have been arranged into three lists, generally known as the "white list," the "gray list" and the "black list." The "white" list sets forth license provisions that would normally be considered trade restrictions, but have been determined by the European

Economic Commission to provide sufficient benefits to merit an exemption. The "gray" list sets forth license provisions that normally would not be considered trade restrictions but which, given certain legal or economic circumstances, may come within the prohibitions of Article 85 of the Treaty of Rome. The "black" list sets forth provisions which are not allowed under Article 85.

The Block Exemption regulations for patent license agreements have been in effect since 1985. The Block Exemption regulations for know-how agreements have been in effect since 1989. Before April of 1996, patents and know-how were governed under separate sets of block exemptions. However, on April 1, 1996, the new regulations of the European Commission concerning technology transfer agreements went into effect. The new regulations combined the two sets of block exemptions for patents and know-how into a single set of exemptions. The new regulations apply to licenses of member states' patents, community patents and European patents, licenses of know-how and combined or hybrid patent and know-how license agreements. The change in the exemptions specifically recognizes that the presence of two separate lists of block exemptions created some confusion because many license agreements include both patents and know-how. The European Commission included a grandfather clause in the regulations for existing agreements, which will still be governed by the previous block exemptions. Agreements currently in force as of April 1 can continue to run provided they fulfill the requirements of the new regulations. The new regulations will expire on March 31, 2005.

One of the most significant changes in the revised exemptions was the introduction of a market share test, allowing the European Commission to withdraw the benefit of a block exemption where the licensed products are not exposed to effective competition within a licensed territory. The Commission noted that it would pay special attention to instances where the licensee has more than a forty percent share of the market, not only for licensed products but for "equivalent products" which were defined as "products or services which customers consider interchangeable or substitutable on account of their characteristics, prices and intended use."

The Commission also has the authority to withdraw an exemption in any agreement which blocks or hinders the free circulation of products offered in the Common Market. Price restrictions are blacklisted, as are quantity restrictions, except if the purpose of the restrictions in the license agreement is to create a second source of supply for a specific customer. In this case, the licensor can limit the licensee to the quantity required by the specific customer. The Commission will also allow the licensor to restrict the licensee to producing quantities required solely for its own purpose.

The regulations also blacklist agreements where a licensee's obligation to produce or use his best efforts to produce a minimum quantity effectively prevents him from using competing technologies. Non-compete provisions in the license agreement are blacklisted. With respect to grant back provisions in license agreements, the revised exemptions provide that a licensee cannot be required to assign improvements or new applications back to the licensor.

It is important to note that it is possible that if a licensor does not expressly grant a right in a license agreement, the European Court of Justice may interpret the agreement as inherently imposing a restriction which denies that right to the licensee. If such a denial brings the agreement outside the scope of the block exemptions, the agreement may be objectionable even if it contains nothing which expressly violates the Treaty of Rome.

In view of the potential difficulties that can occur in attempting to draft the appropriate license agreement, it is always important that experienced European counsel be fully advised of the intentions of the parties to the agreement and be given the opportunity to review the final wording of the proposed document. Further, as the European economic regulations are in a continual period of flux, it is important to obtain a fresh review by both U.S. and European counsel in each case.

Licensing in the Pacific Rim

It is no a secret that one of the keys to Japan's incredible post-World War II industrial success was its ability to make improvements to the technology that it had licensed from the west beginning in the 1950's. Japan's extraordinary success has caused the rest of the industrial world to view the Pacific Rim as both a source of new technology available for licensing in addition to its value as a marketplace for Western goods and technology. This is particularly true in view of the emergence of South Korea, Taiwan and Singapore as economic and technological centers, in no small part due to concerted efforts of their respective governments to encourage such development.

Now, with the relaxation of trade barriers with the Republic of China, the world has its eyes set upon the economic potential of a developed Chinese economy, as well as its one billion potential customers.

The Pacific Rim is clearly one of the most important areas for licensing overseas. Pacific Rim nations currently contain approximately thirty percent of the world's total population, and their combined economies are growing more quickly than most western countries. Those able to exploit this growing market will clearly be able to take advantage of the new "global" economy.

Japan

Japan's current dominant position in the world of technology is beyond question. Perhaps due to the absence of a military machine to fund since the end of the Second World War, Japan has been able to devote its resources to developing itself into an industrial powerhouse that is the envy of the world. This was partly a result of Japan's willingness, since the 1950's, to license western technology, only to find means by which to improve it. Now, the same western countries that once licensed state-of-the art technology to the Japanese are the biggest consumers of Japan's exports.

While Japanese technology is currently in great demand, Japan has not yet lessened its appetite for western technology. However, doing business in Japan requires a different approach than in the United States. One must first understand that the vast cultural differences between Japan and the United States mandate a consideration of Japanese culture as the key to successful negotiation. Failure to understand Japanese culture will ruin the business venture before it even gets off the ground.

First and foremost, it must be recognized that Japan does not subscribe to the western myth of the "rugged individualist," with its strong emphasis on individuality and freedom from social and/or governmental restraint. Japan's social structure, which developed from tribal traditions that remain significant today, aspires conformity as a means to maintain social order. In Japan, the pressure on each individual to uphold his or her own role as a part of the Japanese society is so strong that the Japanese cannot possibly understand the western view that "the law" (read "politicians and lawyers") are somehow necessary to preserve the social order and to prevent chaos. In business, this results in a distinct Japanese distrust of lawyers and their alleged penchant for creating disputes and litigation. In the Japanese view, invoking the "law" in order to resolve a dispute is not viewed favorably. Thus, while it is always advisable to keep the business people in front while conducting the negotiations of a licensing transaction, utilizing the lawyers should be the absolute "last resort" in attempting to resolve a dispute. It is, in fact, advisable to utilize lawyers only when the Japanese counterparts use lawyers. Further, the acute Japanese dislike of litigation makes it advisable to negotiate an agreement which appears to utilize every means possible to avoid litigation in the event of a dispute. Where the willingness to negotiate a dispute might be viewed upon by some Americans as a weakness, the Japanese will appreciate such an effort. Also, because of the uncanny ability of the Japanese to make improvements to Western technology, those licensing technology to the Japanese might want to consider a cross licensing arrangement in order to ensure access to such improvements.

People's Republic of China

With its one billion potential consumers and abundant natural resources, the recent "westernization" of the mainland Chinese economy has attracted considerable attention in the western world. Fueled by China's new appetite for western technology, American companies have been beating paths to China in attempts to take advantage of these potential markets, or to look for Chinese joint venture partners. However, as in Japan, one must be aware of the distinct cultural differences between China and the west in order to have any chance of successfully conclude a business venture in China.

In China, it is said that the most important key to a successful business negotiation is that one must be willing to devote sufficient time and effort to develop trust. In fact, the more personal the relationship, the greater the chance of success. Thus, it is important to approach business negotiations with the goal of developing a friendship as well as a business relationship.

It is also important that all parties to the agreement be absolutely certain that the agreement accurately reflects the understanding of all parties concerned. This may often require the assistance of Chinese advisors, particularly when there may be uncertainties as to how the agreement will operate under Chinese law. In that regard, China shares some of Japan's traditional distrust of lawyers and the legal system.

According to Larry W. Evans of the Chicago law firm of Willain Brinks Hofer Gilson & Lione, one of the country's leading experts on doing business in China, license negotiations with the Chinese tend to follow a formal five-stage pattern. These five stages may be summarized as follows:[1]

1. an introductory phase, where the Chinese negotiators try to learn as much as they can about their western counterparts as well as the technology in question;
2. a discussion of the fundamental structure of the venture and the conclusion of a letter of intent;
3. formal contract negotiations, including the terms of the licenses and a description of the technology transfer process;
4. discussions of the commercial terms of the agreement, including all legal provisions; and
5. discussions concerning price and the manner of payment.

It is said that in China, there will not be any serious negotiations about price until all of the other outstanding issues have been resolved. It is therefore incumbent upon those negotiating on behalf of western companies to demonstrate patience. Western negotiators should keep in mind that developing a successful venture in China will take longer and will be more expensive than in many other nations, and that the price should therefore be adjusted accord-

---

[1] See Evans, Larry, "Licensing in China: A Perspective of a Twenty-Year Veteran," *Licensing Law and Business Report*, March-April 1994 at 207-214.

ingly. Further, Chinese business culture tends to view a contract as a continuously evolving process, which does not conclude with the signing of a formal agreement. This may be a way for the Chinese to test the sincerity of the relationship that has evolved during the initial phases of the negotiation.

When attempting to negotiate a license, it is often advisable to consult a Chinese attorney or other licensing specialist in order to ensure that the agreement is in conformance with the myriad of Chinese trade regulations. For example, current Chinese trade regulations have set a ten-year limit to the payment of royalties, which has caused some licensors to require a lump-sum payment up front. Similarly, it is recommended that the parties acknowledge that the licensed technology is in fact "advanced technology," which will allow the transaction to be viewed upon favorably under the Chinese technology transfer regulations. "Advanced technology," as defined under these regulations, is that which will lead to new product development, expand exports, substitute imports with domestically produced products or satisfy a demand for a product in short supply. Current Chinese trade regulations also prohibit certain practices in a manner similar to American antitrust laws, such as restricting the licensee's distribution channels, prohibiting the licensee from acquiring competitive technology or requiring payment for unusable or invalid patents. These same regulations, the Detailed Rules For Implementing Technology Transfer Contracts by the Ministry of Foreign Economic Relations and Trade, published on January 20, 1988, also detail the specific procedures which must be followed in order to gain governmental approval of license agreements and corresponding technology transfers. Again, it is recommended that local counsel be consulted early during the negotiation process in order to make certain that all regulations are necessarily complied with.

South Korea

While Korea has been able to replicate Japan's success in becoming a true industrial giant, it has not always been easy for foreign companies to conclude license agreements with Korean national companies. Traditionally, it was necessary to obtain prior governmental approval of most technology licenses before the licenses were to go into effect if:

1. the license term was one year or longer and involved a royalty of $300,000 (US) or more; or
2. the license called for an initial payment of more than $50,000 (US) and a royalty of three percent or greater.

Further, it was required to register the license with the Korean Fair Trade Commission (FTC) if the license called for a royalty in excess of two percent or if the term was to be greater than three years and included a lump sum payment in excess of $100,000. Failure to follow theses guidelines would result in severe penalties.

In 1995, a new law was proposed which, if approved, would reduce some of these burdensome regulations. The law eliminates the requirement of advance governmental approval while allowing either party to the prospective license to seek a ruling, either before entering into the agreement or while the agreement is in effect, as to any provision in the license agreement which might be questionable under Korean law. The law will also allow the FTC to publish a list of those practices which are specifically permitted and/or prohibited in order to give the parties a better understanding as to the legality of any proposed licensing provisions. The law will also permit the Korean government to levy fines for violations of the licensing guidelines.

As of this writing, it is uncertain whether this law will be approved, as certain powerful industries have come out in opposition. Many foreign companies are hoping that these provisions will be enacted, as it will advance the opportunities for foreigners to do business in Korea.

At present, there are certain licensing practices which, as in the EEC, are specifically prohibited under Korean law. These provisions include requiring the licensee to grant back a free and exclusive license to any improvements to the licensed property, requiring the payment of royalties after the expiration of the license and licensee estoppel. Other antitrust-related practices which are currently prohibited include a licensor's attempts to restrict the licensee's sales or control its sale and/or distribution methods, export restrictions and requirements that the licensee buy products or take other licenses from the licensor.

With respect to the licensor's obligations, if a licensor warrants the validity of a licensed patent, and the patent is later found to be invalid, Korean law will require the licensor to return all royalties paid under the license. Korean law, which tends to favor the licensee (especially when the licensee is a native entity), also prohibits the licensor from requiring that the licensee indemnify it against actions brought by a third party.

NINE:
Administering the Licensing Program

The role and function of the licensing administrator will depend in large measure on the size and scope of the licensing program and what responsibilities, if any, fall under the umbrella of the administrator. By and large, however, some of the more significant responsibilities of the licensing administrator include:

- identifying the potential licensable properties of the company;
- insuring that all necessary steps have been taken to protect these potentially licensable properties under the applicable intellectual property laws;
- identifying all potential licensees and investigating their capabilities;
- initiating licensing discussions with potential licensees and attempting to conclude licensing negotiations;
- developing a set of license agreements to be used with prospective licensees;
- negotiating the terms and conditions of license agreements with serious licensees;
- coordinating the licensing program and insuring that the company is in full compliance with all of its contractual obligations;

- overseeing the licensee's responsibilities for making full and timely royalty payments;
- overseeing the licensee's non-financial responsibilities to insure that the licensee is in full compliance with all of its contractual obligations;
- developing and working with an audit team to insure that the licensee is in full compliance with its royalty obligations;
- continuing to work with the technical personnel at the company to monitor the development of improvements to the licensed technology;
- insuring that appropriate legal protection is obtained for improvements;
- maintaining a feeling for the marketplace to determine whether any infringements occur with respect to the licensed patents or technology; and
- acting as the interface between licensor and licensee to maintain a good working relationship between the parties.

The above list is not a complete list of all of the administrator's responsibilities but, instead, is intended to identify some of the more important elements of the administrator. Many of these tasks will require legal and patent assistance. Thus, the administrator should be able to interface and work effectively with both inside and outside counsel.

The role and responsibility of a technology licensing manager can be the subject of its own work. In fact, it has been. For an excellent overview of the topic, reference should be made to Robert Goldscheider's book, **Technology Management** published by Clark Boardman Callaghan.

Accountability

At least one licensor has proclaimed, "Every licensee cheats." This is clearly an overstatement and is, no doubt, based more on hyperbole than on fact. Most licensees are honest. Most licensees regularly pay their full royalties every quarter. Most licensees have never thought about cheating their licensors. In actual fact, there are relatively few instances where licensees consciously cheat their licensors.

Nevertheless, licensees do make accounting errors. Licensees do sometimes take improper credits in determining the royalty base. Licensees mistakenly fail to include certain sales in calculating the royalty base. In short, errors do happen, and there are instances where licensors have not received their fair share of royalty income.

Determining Whether a Problem Exists

Most licensors trust their licensees to report sales properly and accurately. Every quarter they receive a royalty statement and a check based on that statement. On its face, the numbers always appear quite correct. Or at least, the numbers add up. There are times, however, when a licensor may begin questioning the correctness of the statements. For example, the licensor may know of sales of the product in markets that do not appear on the royalty statement. Similarly, the licensor may become aware of substantial sales in a particular country that do not appear on the statement. A licensor may believe that a particular item sold well during a particular season only to find the sales were lower than the previous quarter. All of these circumstances make a licensor begin to question whether or not its licensee is accurately reporting the royalty income.

What should a licensor do in these situations? The answer is to speak with an accounting firm or a professional royalty investigator to determine whether a problem truly exists or whether the licensor's paranoia has begun to run rampant.

Royalty Investigations Explained

Most Certified Public Accountant firms do not like to use the term "audit" in conjunction with the examination of a company's books and records to determine whether it has fully paid its royalty obligation. Instead, the phrase "royalty investigation" is typically used to investigate and determine that question. Others have referred to the exercise as an "on-site compliance review." Most laymen and attorneys still call it an audit.

There are a number of excellent accounting firms that have departments that specialize in royalty investigations. Similarly, there are a number of smaller, regional firms that specialize in royalty investigations and will do an excellent job for the licensor. Some of these firms represent a number of different licensors in a particular industry. In fact, they frequently will perform a royalty investigation of a particular manufacturer on behalf of a number of different clients at the same time. This obviously results in lower rates for the clients, since the cost of the investigation is borne by all of the participants. While most accounting firms will only work on an hourly billing rate, there are a handful of independent accountants that will perform royalty investigations on a contingency fee arrangement, in which case they will only receive payment if they are successful in recovering monies for the licensor.

One word of caution is necessary. Royalty investigations can become quite expensive. The licensor should understand the potential costs prior to embarking on such an investigation. More importantly, however, the licensor should be reasonably sure that there are substantial sums of money at issue prior to undertaking an investigation that may cost in the tens of thousands of dollars. Before retaining an accounting firm to perform a royalty investigation, licensors should insure that their agreements afford them the right to conduct such investigations.

Most investigation provisions include the following elements:

- give the licensor the right to conduct the audit on reasonable notice with the right to make copies;
- provide that in the event of an underpayment, the licensee will pay the difference plus interest as well as pay for the cost of the investigation if the underpayment is greater than a threshold amount;
- require the licensee to maintain relevant records for a minimum period of time; and
- require the licensor to preserve the confidentiality of any business information to which the licensor may be exposed.

A typical "audit" provision reads as follows:

(a) LICENSOR shall have the right, upon at least five (5) days written notice and no more than once per calendar year, to inspect

LICENSEE's books and records and all other documents and materials in the possession of or under the control of LICENSEE with respect to the subject matter of this Agreement at the place or places where such records are normally retained by LICENSEE. LICENSOR shall have free and full access thereto for such purpose and shall be permitted to be able to make copies thereof and extracts therefrom.

(b) In the event that such inspection reveals a discrepancy in the amount of Royalty owed LICENSOR from what was actually paid, LICENSEE shall pay such discrepancy, plus interest, calculated at the rate of one percent (1%) per month. In the event that such discrepancy is in excess of Three Thousand United States Dollars ($3,000.00), LICENSEE shall also reimburse LICENSOR for the cost of such inspection including any attorneys' fees incurred in connection therewith.

(c) All books and records relative to LICENSEE's obligations hereunder shall be maintained and kept accessible and available to LICENSOR for inspection for at least three (3) years after termination of this Agreement.

(d) In the event that an investigation of LICENSEE's books and records is made, certain confidential and proprietary business information of LICENSEE may necessarily be made available to the person or persons conducting such investigation. It is agreed that such confidential and proprietary information shall be retained in confidence by LICENSOR and shall not be used by LICENSOR or disclosed to any third party for a period of two (2) years from the date of disclosure, or without the prior express written permission of LICENSEE unless required by law or in connection with any proceeding based on LICENSEE's failure to pay its actual Royalty obligation.

In preparation for the first meeting with the accountants, the licensor should compile all of the royalty statements rendered by the licensee since commencement of sales. Similarly, the licensing administrator should attempt to document all potential inconsistencies of which he or she may be aware. Armed with that information, the licensor should then meet with the accounting firm. In addition to turning all of the above documents and information over to the accountant, the licensor should also provide a copy of the agreement governing the payment of royalties. The accountants will need to refer to that agreement in the course of the royalty investigation.

The Royalty Investigation

The accountants will then contact the licensee and set up an appointment to conduct the investigation. Most licensees have had investigations conducted before and, as such, consider the matter little more than a business inconvenience.

After setting up the appointment, the accountant will send the company a list of the items that he or she will want to review in the course of the investigation. This will include the accounting, sales and manufacturing records of the company relative to the product in question as well as copies of the company's catalog and price lists for the relevant period. The accountant may also ask for all back-up material used to prepare the licensor's royalty statement as well as a list of all company locations including outlet and retail locations.

If the company has all of the requested material on hand at the time the accountant arrives to perform the investigation, it should be a relatively easy procedure, frequently taking no more than a day or two. If not, the procedure may be arduous and the results may be inconclusive. The accountant should be able to make photocopies of the company's books and records as well as extract information. This will permit the accountant to be able to render a complete and meaningful report to the licensor which can then be used against the company if there is any evidence of under-reporting.

The obvious goal of any accountant in conducting a royalty investigation is to compare the licensor's royalty statement against the actual sales records of the company to see whether the company accurately accounted to the licensor. At the conclusion of the royalty investigation, the accountant will then render a formal report to the licensor, comparing the company's manufacturing and sales records against the licensor's royalty statements.

What the Investigation May Reveal

As noted above, most licensees are honest. We live in the age of computers and most of the accounting and sales records of even the smallest companies are computerized. Royalty investigations are common occurrences in virtually all phases of licensing from entertainment to character to technology licensing.

Accordingly, licensees should be prepared for these investigations, and frequently the numbers that the accountant finds reconcile with what the licensee reported to the licensor.

There have, however, been instances where the numbers do not tie out and where it has been found that the licensee has under-reported sales to the licensor, thereby incurring a liability to the licensor for additional royalties. The reasons for under-reporting vary. In virtually all instances, however, the licensee simply made an error.

According to Dan Jacobson in an article that he had written on the subject for *The Licensing Journal*, the most common findings of a royalty investigation are:

> *Mathematical Errors.* Even in this age of computers, clerical and arithmetic errors do occur. Totals may be incorrectly carried over from one schedule to the next, and errors in simple arithmetic do occur.
>
> *Misclassifications.* Another common finding is the misclassification of an item. Was the sales invoice properly coded and posted as the sale of the licensed product? Was the sale misclassified as one bearing a lower royalty rate? Were expenses charged on the statements related to the license? Misclassification of items is commonly found by investigators.
>
> *Incorrect Royalty Base.* The license agreement typically establishes what is to be included in the royalty base and whether the royalty is to be based on list price or wholesale price. The investigator will determine whether the licensee has properly interpreted the contrac-

tual language and applied the correct royalty rate to the right base. Investigators frequently find instances where licensees have used a base for computing royalties which is different from the one permitted under the agreement.

Incorrect Rate. Many agreements provide for changes in royalty rates at differing levels of sale and some provide for different royalty rates in different territories. This is particularly true where there is a domestic royalty rate and an F.O.B. royalty rate. Many accounting errors are attributable to the use of the wrong royalty rate.

Sublicensing. Does the license agreement permit sublicensing? Are the reported royalties based on the sublicensees' sales or on the amounts remitted by the sublicensee to the licensee?

Unaccounted for Production. Some of the most important records from the investigator's viewpoint are the production records and those records that reflect the licensee's purchases and inventory. The investigator will want to know the number of units that were available for sale to determine whether they have been sold or are in inventory. The failure of these records to reconcile may be the basis for a claim.

Affiliated Companies. Are sales to affiliates and related parties made at arms length prices? Often, a claim may arise for sales made to a related company at a special price resulting in an under-payment of royalties to the licensor.

Non-Contractual Deductions. The investigator will verify that deductions made by the licensee are provided for in the license agreement. Licensees will occasionally take deductions that are not permitted under the agreement.

Returns and Reserves. The investigator will verify that only actual returns have been deducted from the royalty statement. Occasionally, a licensee will set up a reserve for returns when only actual returns are permitted under the agreement.

Termination Period. If the term of the agreement has expired, has the licensee stopped manufacturing licensed products as required by the agreement? Has the licensee sold the licensed goods beyond the sell-off period?

Whether or Not to Investigate

After fully understanding the mechanics of a royalty investigation, the licensor must make the difficult decision of whether the send in their accountants to conduct the investigation. Two thoughts cross the licensor's mind: (1) will the company be offended? and (2) does it make business sense to have an investigation conducted?

The licensor should quickly discount the first question. Professional licensors such as the Walt Disney Company retain teams of auditing personnel who regularly conduct these royalty investigations throughout the world. Virtually every major licensor regularly investigates its licensees. Why should you be any different?

By and large, licensees will not blink when they receive the licensor's request to have a royalty investigation conducted. While they may deem such an investigation to be a business inconvenience, they recognize that investigations have become a way of life. For many licensors, these royalty investigations are a regular business practice simply to insure that their licensees have honestly and accurately reported royalty income.

Accordingly, licensors should not concern themselves as to whether such a request will negatively impact their relationship with the company. It should not. On the off chance, however, that such a request might offend a particular company, licensors should ask themselves whether they really want to be doing business with that company in the future.

The second consideration is a much more relevant factor. Royalty investigations are expensive. The cost of a single investigation can easily run into the five figures, although there are ways to reduce the cost, i.e., join in with a group of other licensors for a common investigation or retain a contingent fee investigator. Nevertheless, the licensor runs the risk of incurring substantial expenses with merely the hope of eventually recovering any unpaid royalties. While the license agreement may provide for reimbursement of costs by the company if the investigation reveals an underpayment of a certain amount, the licensor is betting that the investigation will uncover that minimum amount. The licensor should consider having a royalty investigation if:

1. the licensor has evidence or a strong belief that the licensee is underreporting on sales of the licensed products;

2. the earned royalties for the product in question are sufficiently high to justify the cost of such an investigation; or
3. the cost of conducting the investigation is sufficiently low so as to justify the investigation as a regular business practice.

TEN:
Special Forms of Licensing

This chapter will provide a brief overview of two of the newest and most active areas in technology licensing: biotechnology and multimedia licensing. These areas typically involve emerging technologies from a number of disciplines. As a result, the license agreements which cover these technologies tend to depart from the traditional licensing norms and procedures that have been discussed thus far. This chapter intends to discuss some of the basic differences that parties negotiating these types of licensing agreements may encounter and some of the unique issues which must be addressed.

Biotechnology

During the 1980's, the hottest field in technology licensing was biotechnology. Biotechnology, which can broadly be defined as the development of unique products or results through the use of recombinant DNA and associated recombinant technology in living organisms (man, animal or plant), was introduced as a methodology which could solve the world's medical problems. Biotechnological processes could create new and better food products through the genetic modification of plants. As a result of these claims, companies large and small rushed to create new biotechnology divisions within their own organizations or to enter into strategic alliances with universities or with one of the dynamic new biotechnology companies that seemed to appear almost overnight.

Today, the dust has settled and ten year's worth of reality has shaped the marketplace. Those who feared that biotechnology was going to create a new race of Frankenstein monsters have gone the way of angry villagers of days past. Those who were afraid of the health and philosophical consequences of a genetically-altered tomato seem to have had little to fear. Still, while "multimedia" may have replaced biotechnology as the hot button of technology licensing, biotechnology licensing remains viable and dynamic. While these companies are no longer front page news, there are approximately 1,300 bona-fide biotechnology companies in the United States alone, continuing to engage in valuable research and licensing activities, with significant research and development taking place on the nation's university campuses as well.

The Biotech Alliances of Today and Tomorrow

One of the most important lessons that was learned over the last decade was that the larger pharmaceutical companies, many of whom had rushed to create new biotechnology divisions, have now come to understand that their research divisions may not be as well suited for new types of research as they might have been when they were smaller, younger companies. As such, they have come to value licensing alliances with the smaller biotechnology companies, who in turn have come to realize that they lack the resources to become a fully integrated international maker and seller of products. Both types of companies have their own resources to bring to the biotech bargaining table. The smaller biotechnology companies seem to be very good at producing new technology and developing new product ideas, while the pharmaceutical companies, by and large, have the financial resources to develop those ideas into a viable, marketable product.

Similarly, the valuable research taking place at universities is also being utilized by the private sector. It is not uncommon for a corporation to go to a university or research laboratory and agree to sponsor research in a particular area in exchange for a license to the work product that is developed. In the alternative, companies will directly approach the university to license particular technology.

As noted above, one of the main reasons smaller biotechnology companies ally themselves with larger and more financially sound companies is the sheer economic reality of bringing a product to the market. According to some, the cost of taking a product from concept through the entire regulatory process to approval in the pharmaceutical industry can be in the hundreds of millions of dollars. The manufacture of some biotechnology products also requires special equipment and facilities, which significantly add to the capital costs of bringing a product to market. Thus, while a biotechnology license may resemble a more traditional technology license with respect to terms such as territorial and geographic limitations, the agreement may shift more of the financial burden to the licensee than in other types of technology licenses. In addition to these costs, it is not uncommon for a biotechnology agreement to provide that the licensee be responsible for the costs of obtaining and maintaining patent protection for the product, because many smaller biotechnology companies simply do not have the resources to divert from research and development.

Creative Compensation Structures

As such, the overall structure as well as the compensation aspects of a biotechnology license agreement may be more complex. In more traditional technology licensing, the licensor receives the majority of its revenue in the form of royalties. In the biotechnology industry, the notion of getting a royalty stream starting at the end of the drug development cycle, which can be as long as eight or ten years, is unsatisfactory to justify the huge capital costs which are invested up front. Therefore, biotechnology companies are willing to trade future royalties for up-front money. This can be in the form of a signing fee which may reflect the development costs incurred to date. Thus, the relationship may be less of a traditional licensor-licensee relationship and be more akin to a joint venture, although not in the sense where an independent third entity is created. In this way, the biotech relationship resembles a corporate partnership, where the parties share tasks and responsibilities in many different ways and forms.

Another form of compensation occurs when the licensee is willing to support the research, but is not convinced that it will lead to a viable, marketable product. In this situation, the licensee may not want to pay any fees up front, but is willing to pay once there are tangible results of the research. Accordingly, the licensee may agree to pay based upon a set number of research milestones designed to limit its outlay of funds until such time that it has a reasonable basis to believe that the project will in fact succeed.

Royalty Determinations

Another form of compensation to be considered in setting up a biotechnology license agreement is the equity investment approach. In some instances, a licensee agrees to purchase stock in the biotechnology company in order to provide the latter with sufficient capital to maintain its development process. As a practical matter, this is an effective way of spreading the risk among many of the end products of a particular company, with out "putting all of its eggs in one basket."

Notwithstanding the above, there are situations where compensation in biotechnology licenses are set up as in other more traditional technology licensing arrangements, with advances, minimum royalties and a fixed royalty percentage. Oftentimes, the royalty rate may be tied into a sliding scale depending on volume, although the question of whether the scale slides up or down with volume will depend upon the economics of the particular process. As touched on elsewhere in this book, it would be wonderful if royalty rates in biotechnology licenses could themselves be reduced into some magic formula that the parties could simply plug into a particular situation. Regrettably, this is not possible. Putting a price tag on a product and breaking the price down is as difficult in biotechnology as in other disciplines, and maybe even more so. The cost of the research is always an important factor, particularly in the eyes of the developer. Yet, the first approach may still be for the parties to examine a percentage of the estimate of the licensee's margin of profit of the end product, and try to negotiate a royalty between six to twelve percent. License agreements with universities tend to involve lower royalty rates, as the licensee often requires additional technology to develop the product.

Clearly, the patentability of the end product of a biotechnology agreement is an important issue in trying to determine an acceptable compensation structure. However, the inherent difficulty in biotechnology research is that at the time the license is consummated, the parties may not really know what the end product is going to be, and likely, the patent is not even issued on the technology. Furthermore, patent protection in this industry can be a long and costly process. Thus, even though the end product may be patentable, it is difficult to utilize the potential patentability of a product as a major factor in trying to place a value on the licensed property when setting up a compensation structure.

Enforcing the Intellectual Property Rights

In negotiating biotechnology licenses, the issue of who will bear the responsibility and costs for enforcing the intellectual property rights in the product and for defending accusations of patent infringement by third parties are extremely important. Traditionally, the technology licensor is required to enforce its patent or accept reduced royalties if it refuses to stop an unlicensed party from competing with its licensee. In the biotechnology area, sometimes the licensee will insist upon the right to enforce the property, in part because of its greater financial stake in the project as well as its greater skill, experience and resources in conducting litigation. However, many licensors do not want to relinquish their rights because they believe that the application of the licensed technology may go beyond what they have licensed, and therefore may believe they have a greater interest in defending their patent rights.

In developing and negotiating a biotechnology license, it is important to recognize that licensing of biotechnology products may be more complex than in many other technical fields, as each transaction involves patent consideration, contract/licensing considerations and FDA regulation of the end product. The FDA impacts not only how a product gets to the marketplace but what the product actually consists of when it enters the marketplace. For example, by the time the product label information is approved, it may or may not have any correlation with the claims of the patent or the way the parties believed it would turn out when they entered into the license agreement. This must, therefore, be considered when defining the licensed technology in the agreement.

Notwithstanding the above, the biotechnology field continues to present a multitude of valuable licensing opportunities, particularly as more biotechnology companies become less insistent on attempting to develop into fully integrated worldwide makers and sellers of products. As such, they may be far more inclined to give up manufacturing rights or the right to conduct clinical trials in the United States with respect to more of their products than they had historically been. This can lead to a more "traditional" approach to developing a license agreement, as the parties may no longer be arguing about who will retain the biotech rights. This has, in turn, permitted the large drug and pharmaceutical companies to become more familiar with the special needs of the biotechnology companies, thereby allowing the parties to focus more on the economics of the transaction.

International Considerations

It has become much easier to form international biotechnology license agreements since the fall of the Soviet Union. Previously, technology export regulations had been more strict because of the fear that biotechnology products might fall into the wrong hands and be transformed into weapons. While not nearly as stringent as before, export controls remain, as does the overall concern that the technology is not passed on from the licensee's country to unlicensed third parties. As touched on elsewhere in this book, other issues of concern to technology licensors, such as the availability of hard currency, the fear that the royalties will be impounded by foreign governments and concerns about the tendencies of some foreign governments to withhold taxes on payments earned overseas, apply to the biotechnology area as well.

Other important aspects of negotiating an overseas biotechnology license agreements include the issue of where the parties agree to litigate a potential dispute either under the license agreement or patents that may relate thereto, as well as what language and what set of rules will apply. In addition, as touched on elsewhere in this volume, the regulations of the European Economic Community must be considered, as current regulations may prevent a licensor from placing restrictions on a licensee's ability to sell beyond its borders into other member countries. In that regard, it is always important to consult overseas counsel in order to determine if any of the so-called "block exemptions" apply.

Multimedia*

"Multimedia" is a word that seems to have emerged virtually simultaneously in the popular, technical, and legal vocabularies. Scores of newspaper articles have been written about it, magazines for computer users are filled with detailed discussions and evaluations of multimedia hardware and software, and the desire of members of the legal profession to attend countless seminars on the legal implications and problems of multimedia is seemingly unquenchable. But what is it?

Multimedia Defined

"Multimedia" means, most simply, more than one media. It is a concept that, at least at the surface level, is intuitive and easily understood. We live, after all, in a multimedia world in which we receive constant input through a wide range of media — through sight and sound, through smell and taste, and touch. In a broad and literal sense, you have a multimedia expericncc when you walk down the street on a spring day, feel the warm sun on your skin, and smell the flowers in bloom, while listening to a Sony Walkman and eating a chocolate chip cookie.

Electronic multimedia, at least conceptually, is not much different. My own view is that, consistent with the broad, real-life multimedia that each of us experiences everyday, electronic multimedia in the sense that we are speaking of here should be broadly

---

* The authors would like to thank Craig Blakeley for preparing this section on multimedia. Mr. Blakeley is associated with the law firm of Gordon & Glickson P.C. in Washington, DC.

defined — it involves some combination of more than one type of conventional or electronic media presented through an electronic or computational interface. Thus, although most electronic multimedia will have some processing or computing component, I do not believe that a computer is a necessary element of all electronic multimedia. Similarly, although some have urged that true multimedia must contain some type of telecommunications element, there are a wide range of stand-alone multimedia applications in which the only interaction or interactivity occurs between the user and the computer, with no communications function beyond that.

A few examples will serve to illustrate my point. If as a starting point, we adopt the simple, but straightforward concept that multimedia means more than one media, it is apparent that multimedia services abound, albeit many in rudimentary form. The home shopping services that are carried on cable and over-the-air television are examples of basic multimedia services. They rely upon orders from viewers communicated by telephone (another media) in order to sell products. Although they are not truly interactive (in the sense that the viewer cannot place his order by using the same electronic pathway that was used to transmit the program to the viewer), because a combination of two media, television and telephone, is necessary for the service to function, home shopping is, indeed, a multimedia service.

Multimedia in the Computer Industry

A more sophisticated type of multimedia that exists now and will come into increasing use in the future is that provided via a stand-alone computer combined with a CD-ROM player or other type of data storage device. This has the capability to furnish the user with a combination of textual, visual and audio output which may be manipulable by the user through the computer interface. For example, imagine an entry concerning John Lennon in an electronic encyclopedia contained on a CD-ROM. As in a conventional, printed encyclopedia, there will be a textual description and biography of John Lennon — this can be viewed on the screen by the user or printed. However, a multimedia encyclopedia will offer more than simply a dry, unadorned textual description. The user might be able, while reading the text, to pull up photographs of John Lennon, read newspaper articles about his death, view portions of motion pictures or videos in which John Lennon appeared, and, of course, listen to some of his music. Such an encyclopedic entry will appear different to each user based upon the user's ability to focus on those aspects of Lennon's life in which he or she is most interested. Utilizing the capabilities of the computer interface, the user also may have the ability to create an individualized description or biography of Lennon, drawing upon the basic elements included in the encyclopedia. Such an electronic encyclopedia is truly multimedia and poses a broad range of potential legal issues, some of which are touched on below.

Interactive Multimedia

Another kind of electronic multimedia is broadband, interactive multimedia of the type that many envision will be provided over the so-called "Information Superhighway." One possible vision of the future of telephone communications is a personal phone number associated with an individual, rather than a geographic location, and which moves with that individual as he or she travels from the home, to an automobile, to the office, to an airport, etc. The ultimate progeny of the first group of Personal Digital Assistants, such as Apple's Newton, may well be a small, compact, highly portable computer/fax terminal/telephone associated with a personal telephone number, interconnected with the rest of the world on a wireless basis through radio frequencies, and on which the user will have the flexibility to receive, send and manipulate textual, visual, aural and other types of data. This, too, is multimedia.

"Virtual Reality"

In its most advanced and futuristic form (at least as we now can envision it), electronic multimedia would be a "virtual reality" which, through its input to our various senses, would be virtually indistinguishable from the real thing — such as the springtime walk with which I began this section. As illustrated by these examples, at the "micro" level the range of potential multimedia applications and products is broad, indeed. Equally broad is the scope of social, political, economic and legal problems that are raised potentially by such applications.

For example, as the range of available shop-at-home services multiplies, there will be a strong temptation for those companies to accumulate unified databases on individuals or households that contain information on credit, income and buying preferences. Aside from exposing already saturated consumers to even more advertising, precisely calibrated to individual lifestyles and incomes, such interrelational databases may expose us to unwelcome scrutiny by the government as well as by unscrupulous private entities. I believe that privacy issues, particularly those posed by interactive multimedia applications, will be a large and growing concern flowing from electronic multimedia.

Intellectual property issues also loom very large on the multimedia horizon. Indeed, if not resolved, some of these problems could prevent multimedia from reaching its full potential. For instance, take my example of the entry in the electronic encyclopedia concerning John Lennon. Writing a textual description of Lennon's life is no problem — with proper attribution to the applicable sources, anyone with some time and effort could assemble a serviceable biography. But what about the photographs, the newspaper articles, the movies and the music? The rights to those are held by a variety of individuals and entities. How does the assembler of a multimedia product identify the rights and the rights holders? How does the assembler obtain the necessary permissions from the rights holders? How should those rights be valued? Do the rights licensed to the assembler of a multimedia product include the derivative right to the end user to reassemble and restructure the component parts of that product? If multimedia is to get off the ground, these and other intellectual property issues must be resolved.

Legal Issues

Indeed, some, such as Dan Brenner of the National Cable Television Association, have suggested that a system of compulsory licensing should be adopted, either voluntarily or, if necessary, by governmental fiat, in order to ensure that the difficulties inherent in assembling these rights through private negotiation do not cripple the development of multimedia.

Multimedia issues do not stop at the "micro" level. There are also overarching, structural and regulatory issues that must be faced on the "macro" level and that, at least to some degree, are a result of the problems associated with developing "micro" multimedia products. Thus, the need to assemble the necessary intellectual property rights may drive software developers and distributors to seek strategic alliances or combinations with rights holders. After all, if you own the necessary rights, there is no need to engage in complex and expensive negotiations in order to obtain them. Software suppliers will seek the same type of alliances or combinations with distributors. Distributors, on the other hand, may attempt to develop their own software or content, rather than licensing the rights from someone else.

Such cross-media deals necessarily will raise antitrust, economic, and political issues as regulators seek to balance concerns about the preservation and encouragement of competition with a recognition of the efficiencies and economies of scale that may result from those combinations. Thus, the now moribund Bell Atlantic/TCI deal and QVC's unsuccessful quest for Paramount are also, in my view, within the scope of issues that must be considered as we enter the age of multimedia.

Conclusion

Multimedia is a broad concept that must be examined at both the "micro" and "macro" levels and which, by its very nature, is ever-changing. It would be a mistake if, in trying to deal with this important new technology, we try to pigeonhole it into a narrow regulatory or legal classification. We must recognize that a flexible and creative approach is needed in order to deal successfully with a synthetic new media that is inherently dynamic. Although current intellectual and legal paradigms may be useful starting places for the required analysis, these well-worn analytical tools were developed in response to older, less complex, technologies. There may well be a need to develop new legal and regulatory models to ensure that the constraints of the past do not prevent multimedia from achieving its full and enormous potential in the future.

Appendix One:
List of Resources

1. Associations

- American Intellectual Property Law Association (AIPLA)
  2001 Jefferson Davis Highway, Suite 203
  Arlington, VA 22202
  Telephone: (703) 415-0780

- American Bar Association – Intellectual Property Law Section
  Chicago, IL
  Telephone: (312) 988-5000

- Association of Corporate Patent Counsel (ACPC)
  Rochester, NY
  Telephone: (716) 724-4437

- International Trademark Association (INTA)
  1133 Avenue of the Americas
  New York, NY 10036-6710
  Telephone: (212) 768-9887

- Licensing Executives Society International (LES)
  1800 Diagonal Road, Suite 280
  Alexandria, VA 22314-2840
  Telephone: (703) 836-3106

2. Publications

Books

- AN OVERVIEW OF INTELLECTUAL PROPERTY: WHAT IS A PATENT, TRADEMARK OR COPYRIGHT, published by the American Intellectual Property Law Association

- INTELLECTUAL PROPERTY INFRINGEMENT DAMAGES, Russell L. Parr, John Wiley & Sons, Inc.

- INTELLECTUAL PROPERTY: LICENSING & JOINT VENTURE PROFIT STRATEGIES, Gordon V. Smith and Russell L. Parr, John Wiley & Sons, Inc.

- INVESTING IN INTANGIBLE ASSETS: FINDING AND PROFITING FROM HIDDEN CORPORATE VALUE, Russell L. Parr, John Wiley & Sons, Inc.

- MULTIMEDIA AND TECHNOLOGY LICENSING AGREEMENTS: FORMS AND COMMENTARY (WITH FORMS ON DISK), Gregory J. Battersby and Charles W. Grimes, Warren, Gorham & Lamont

- VALUATION OF INTELLECTUAL PROPERTY & INTANGIBLE ASSETS - SECOND EDITION, Gordon V. Smith and Russell L. Parr, John Wiley & Sons, Inc.

- TECHNOLOGY LICENSING STRATEGIES, Russell L. Parr and Patrick H. Sullivan, John Wiley & Sons, Inc.

- THE ROYALTY RATE REPORT FOR THE PHARMACEUTICAL & BIOTECHNOLOGY INDUSTRIES, Russell L. Parr, In-

List of Resources / Appendices

tellectual Property Research Associates, Yardley, Pennsylvania.

- THE ROYALTY RATE REPORT FOR THE MEDICAL PRODUCTS INDUSTRY, Russell L. Parr, Intellectual Property Research Associates, Yardley, Pennsylvania.

Periodicals

- *Licensing Economics Review*, 155 Gaither Drive, Moorestown, NJ 08057-1050

- *The Licensing Journal*, Kent Communications, Ltd., P.O. Box 1169, Stamford, CT 06904-1169

- *Multimedia and Technology Licensing Law Report*, Warren, Gorham & Lamont, 395 Hudson Street, New York, NY 10014

Appendix Two:
List of Technology Management Consultants

ANSELL INTERNATIONAL
    345 N. Jackson Street, Suite 209
    Glendale, CA 91206
    Telephone: (818) 247-2698
    Telephone: (818) 507-7921
    Contact: Murray D. Ansell

ARTHUR D. LITTLE ENTERPRISES, INC.
    15 Acorn Park
    Cambridge, MA 02140
    Telephone: (617) 498-5256
    Telefax: (617) 498-7025
    Contact: Daniel Coriat

BANNER & ALLEGRETTI, LTD.
    10 South Wacker Drive, Suite 3000
    Chicago, IL 60606
    Telephone: (312) 715-1000
    Telefax: (312) 715-1234
    Contact: W. Dennis Drehkoff

BARRIGAR & MOSS
Box 49131, 595 Burrard Street
Vancouver, BC V7X 1J1
Canada
Telephone: (604) 689-9255
Telefax: (604) 689-9265
Contact: R. Barrigar

BARRINGTON CONSULTING GROUP, THE
1114 Avenue of the Americas, 30th Floor
New York, NY 10036
Telephone: (212) 819-9300
Telefax: (212) 819-9818
Contact: Joseph A. Agiato

BERNSTEIN & ASSOCIATES
30 Perimeter Center East, Suite 121
Atlanta, GA 30346-1902
Telephone: (770) 671-1755
Telefax: (770) 671-1161
Contact: Jason A. Bernstein

BIO-BUSINESS DEVELOPMENT
203 Garden Place
Radnor, PA 19807
Telephone: (610) 971-9593
Telefax: (610) 964-1320
Contact: Jack Lief

BLAKE TECHNOLOGIES, LTD.
1 West 67th Street, Suite 410
New York, NY 10023
Telephone: (212) 580-2272
Telefax: (212) 595-4278
Contact: Joseph R. Flicek, President

BURDICK & ASSOCIATES
226 E. Broadway
Alton, IL 62002
Telephone: (618) 462-3450
Telefax: (618) 462-7132
Contact: Bruce E. Burdick

BUSINESS VENTURE INVESTMENTS
1720 W. Mountain Avenue
Fort Collins, CO 80521
Telephone: (303) 877-0417
Telefax: 9303) 727-4369
Contact: Warren Hyland

BUSKOP LAW GROUP
1818 Memorial
Houston, TX 77007
Telephone: (713) 862-5035
Telefax: (713) 862-4262
Contact: Ruth Giernhart

COOPERS & LYBRAND
203 North LaSalle Street
Chicago, IL 60601
Telephone: (312) 701-5828
Telefax: (312) 701-6539
Contact: Aron Levko

EAST/WEST TECHNOLOGY PARTNERS, LTD.
1228 31st Street, NW, Suite #2
Washington, DC 20007
Telephone: (202) 338-0902
Telefax: (202) 625-2020
Contact: Mark Taylor, Vice President

EKMS, INC.
100 Inman Street
Cambridge, MA 02139
Telephone: (617) 864-4706
Telefax: (617) 864-7956
Contact: Edward Kahn

FALCO-ARCHER, INC.
20210 NE 116th Street
Redmond, WA 98053
Telephone: (206) 881-6951
Telefax: (206) 881-7194
Contact: Greg Galloway

FIBONACCI, INC.
156 Gallinson Drive
Murray Hill, NJ 07974
Telephone: (908) 464-8295
Telefax: (980) 464-3182
Contact: John C. Bonacci, Ph.D., P.E., U.S. Patent Agent

GERARD A. BLAUFARB, TECHNOLOGY TRANSFER CONSULTANT
433 Yerba Buena Avenue
Los Alto, CA 94022
Telephone: (415) 841-4124
Telefax: (415) 948-0875
Contact: Gerard A. Blaufarb

INTERCON RESEARCH ASSOCIATES LTD.
6565 Lincoln Avenue
Lincolnwood, IL 60646-2644
Telephone: (847) 982-1100
Telefax: (847) 982-1115
Contact: James D. Donovan, President

LAHIVE & COCKFIELD
60 State Street, 5th Floor
Boston, MA 02109
Telephone: (617) 227-7400
Telefax: (617) 227-5941
Contact: Beth E. Arnold, Esq.

MODA INTERNATIONAL MARKETING, INC.
441 Lexington Avenue, Suite 1408
New York, NY 10017
Telephone: (212) 687-7640
Telefax: (212) 687-7942
Contact: Michelle Alfandari

NEW TECHNOLOGY VENTURES, INC.
7649 S.W. 34th Street
Oklahoma City, OK 73179
Telephone: (405) 745-7800
Telefax: (405) 745-2276
Contact: Floyd E. Farha

NEWPORT INTERTRADE
2915 Carob Street
Newport Beach, CA 92660
Telephone: (714) 644-6509
Telefax: (714) 644-4660
Contact: John W. Baldridge

POLLOCK, VANDE SANDE & PRIDDY
Post Office Box 19088
Washington, DC 20036
Telephone: (202) 331-7111
Telefax: (202) 293-6229
Contact: Townsend M. Belser, Jr.

R.D. GILLIS COMPANY
P.O. Box 25123
Shawnee Mission, KS 66225-5123
Telephone: (9130 491-0572
Telefax: (913) 491-3569
Contact: Bob Gillis

SAGE GROUP, THE
245 Route 22 West, Suite 304
Bridgewater, NJ 08807
Telephone: (908) 231-9644
Telefax: (908) 231-9692
Contact: R. Douglas Hulse

STRATECON
5215 Mountain View Road
Winston-Salem, NC 27104-5117
Telephone: (910) 768-6808
Telefax: (910) 765-5149
Contact: Charles I. Beck, Ph.D.

TECHNOLOGY PROPERTIES LTD.
4010 Moorpark Ave., Ste. 215
San Jose, CA 95117
Telephone: (408) 243-9898
Telefax: (408) 296-6637
Contact: D. Mac Leckrone, Licensing Executive

TRADEMARK & LICENSING ASSOCIATES, INC.
7342 Girard Avenue
La Jolla, CA 92037
Telephone: (619) 454-9091
Telefax: (619) 454-7818
Contact: Weston Anson

VENTURE INSIGHTS GROUP
31 North Valley Road
Ridgefield, CT 06877
Telephone: (203) 431-4426
Telefax: (203) 431-6581
Contact: B.I. "Woody" Friedlander

Appendix Three:
Sample Confidential Disclosure Agreement

This Agreement is made as of the **[date]** between **[name of Inventor]**, a **[type of organization]** with offices at **[address]** ("INVENTOR"), and **[name of Company]**, a **[type of organization]** with offices at **[address]** ("COMPANY").

WITNESSETH:

WHEREAS, INVENTOR and COMPANY mutually desire to engage in discussions that may lead to a business relationship; and

WHEREAS, the parties in the course of their dealings may furnish to each other Confidential Information as defined in Paragraph One, and do not wish to convey any interest or copyright therein to the other or make such Confidential Information public or common knowledge;

NOW, THEREFORE, in consideration of the joint nature of the disclosure and the business relationship between the parties, it is hereby agreed as follows:

1. CONFIDENTIAL INFORMATION

For purposes of this agreement, the term "Confidential Information" shall mean the following:

A. Any information, know-how, data, process, technique, design, drawing, program, formula or test data, work in process, engineering, manufacturing, marketing, financial, sales, supplier, customer, employee, investor, or business information, whether in oral, written, graphic, or electronic form; or

B. Any document, diagram, drawing, computer program, or other communication which is either conspicuously marked "confidential", known or reasonably known by the other party to be confidential, or is of a proprietary nature, and is learned or disclosed in the course of discussions, studies, or other work undertaken between the parties.

Anything contrary to the above notwithstanding, Confidential Information shall not include Non-protected Information as defined in Paragraph 5.

2. NONDISCLOSURE

Both INVENTOR and COMPANY and their respective employees and agents agree that during the period of their discussions and/or business relationship, and for a period of [number] years after the later of the termination of such discussions or termination of such relationship, the recipient of Confidential Information will not at any time disclose to any person, or use for its own benefit or the benefit of anyone, Confidential Information of the other party without the prior express written consent of said party.

3. CONSULTANTS

Prior to disclosure of any Confidential Information received by it from the other, the recipient will obtain from all consultants it retains a written agreement: (a) to hold all Confidential Information in confidence and not to use such information for any purpose except as it relates to discussions between the parties or any subsequent business relationship between the parties, and (b) to return all Confidential Information received immediately after consultant has completed its work to the party from whom said information was received.

4. RETURN OF CONFIDENTIAL INFORMATION

The parties agree to promptly deliver to the other any documents reflecting Confidential Information and any copies made thereof that the recipient of said information may have made, may have access to, or may receive or possess during the period of its discussions and/or business relationship. Upon termination of the discussions and/or business relationship between the parties, the recipient of Confidential Information shall promptly deliver to the other party any and all such information in its possession or under its control, except as the parties by prior express written permission or agreement have agreed to retain.

5. NON-PROTECTED INFORMATION

The parties agree that their mutual covenant not to disclose Confidential Information shall not apply to any information or data or other materials imparted to the extent that any of the following conditions exist or come into existence:

A. Information that, at the time access is gained, is already in the recipient's possession or available to it or its employees from any other source having no obligation to the party that is the source of said information.

B. Such information that is, or any time hereafter becomes, available to the public.

C. Such information that, after access is gained to the disclosure, is at any time obtained by the recipient from any other person, firm or company having no obligation to or relationship with the source of said information.

6. COURT-ORDERED DISCLOSURE

Neither INVENTOR nor COMPANY shall be liable for disclosure of Confidential Information if made in response to a valid order of a court or authorized agency of government; provided that ten days' notice first be given to the other party so a protective order, if appropriate, may be sought by such party.

7. NO CONVEYANCE OR LICENSE

Nothing in this Agreement shall be construed to convey to the recipient of Confidential Information any right, title, interest, or copyright in any Confidential Information, or any license to use, sell, exploit, copy, or further develop any such Confidential Information. This Agreement does not in any way bind the parties to enter into a business relationship with the other of any type.

8. JURISDICTION AND DISPUTES

A. This Agreement shall be governed in accordance with the laws of **[state]**.

B. All disputes hereunder shall be resolved in the applicable state or federal courts of **[state]**. The parties consent to the jurisdiction of such courts, agree to accept service of process by mail, and waive any jurisdictional or venue defenses otherwise available.

9. AGREEMENT BINDING ON SUCCESSORS

This Agreement shall be binding upon and shall inure to the benefit of the parties hereto, and their heirs, administrators, successors, and assigns.

10. WAIVER

No waiver by either party of any default shall be deemed as a waiver of any prior or subsequent default of the same or other provisions of this Agreement.

11. SEVERABILITY

If any provision hereof is held invalid or unenforceable by a court of competent jurisdiction, such invalidity shall not affect the validity or operation of any other provision, and such invalid provision shall be deemed to be severed from the Agreement.

12. ASSIGNABILITY

This Agreement is personal to both parties and may not be assigned by any act of either party or by operation of law unless in connection with a transfer of substantially all the assets of such party or with the consent of the other party.

13. INTEGRATION

This Agreement constitutes the entire understanding of the parties, and revokes and supersedes all prior agreements between the parties and is intended as a final expression of their Agreement. It shall not be modified or amended except in writing signed by the parties hereto and specifically referring to this Agreement. This Agreement shall take precedence over any other documents that may be in conflict therewith.

IN WITNESS WHEREOF, this agreement has been duly executed by the parties hereto as of the latest date set forth below.

INVENTOR   COMPANY

By: _____   By: _____
Title: _____   Title: _____
Date: _____   Date: _____

APPENDIX FOUR:
Sample Consulting Agreement for the Technical Consultant

This Agreement is made as of this **[date]** by and between **[name of Consultant]**, a **[type of organization]** with offices at **[address]** ("CONSULTANT"), and **[name of Company]**, a **[type of organization]** with offices at **[address]** ("COMPANY").

WITNESSETH:

WHEREAS, CONSULTANT possesses certain technical expertise in the field **[of computer programming and, in particular, the creation and development of video games]** ("Field");

WHEREAS, COMPANY desires to engage CONSULTANT to perform certain professional consulting services as hereinafter defined in Field; and

WHEREAS, CONSULTANT is willing and able to provide such consulting services to COMPANY in Field.

NOW, THEREFORE, in consideration of the mutual promises and covenants herein contained, the parties hereto agree as follows:

1. RETENTION OF CONSULTANT

A. COMPANY hereby retains the services of CONSULTANT to provide professional consulting services to COMPANY in the Field during the Term of this Agreement. In this regard, CONSULTANT shall advise and assist COMPANY in the creation and development of new products in the Field including, but not limited to, the development of a video game entitled **[name of Product]** ("GAME").

B. CONSULTANT is an independent contractor and not an employee of COMPANY. Unless otherwise expressly agreed to in writing, CONSULTANT shall not be entitled to or eligible for any benefits or programs otherwise given by COMPANY to its employees.

C. CONSULTANT agrees to use the services of **[name]** ("Lead Consultant") on a full-time basis on this project. It is understood and agreed that Lead Consultant will devote substantially all of his or her time and effort to the development of Game.

2. TERM OF THE AGREEMENT

A. The consulting period shall extend from **[date]** through and including **[date]** ("Term"), unless sooner terminated as provided herein.

B. COMPANY shall have the option of renewing the subject Agreement for an additional **[number]**-month period ("Extended Term") on the same terms and conditions as provided for herein by providing CONSULTANT written notice of its intention to renew this Agreement at least **[number]** days prior to the expiration of the Term.

3. OBLIGATIONS OF CONSULTANT

A. Utilizing its own facilities and equipment, CONSULTANT shall be responsible for the creation and development of Game in accordance with a time schedule to be mutually agreed to between the parties. It is, however, anticipated that CONSULTANT will devote at least **[number]** hours per week during the Term to the professional services required of him or her hereunder. Upon agreement from time to time between COMPANY and CONSULTANT, CONSULTANT's hours may be varied to suit the mutual convenience of CONSULTANT and COMPANY.

B. CONSULTANT shall regularly meet with and advise COMPANY on technical matters in Field as well as regularly suggest solutions to technical problems in connection with COMPANY's programs as they may develop.

4. COMPENSATION

A. In full consideration for the services being rendered by CONSULTANT hereunder, COMPANY agrees to pay CONSULTANT during the Term of this Agreement a consulting fee in the amount of **[amount]** U.S. Dollars ($___) per **[time period]** ("Consulting Fee"). Consulting Fee shall be paid on **a [time period]** basis within **[number]** days after the conclusion of each **[time period]**.

B. CONSULTANT shall be responsible for all ordinary and reasonable expenses that it may incur in connection with this project. COMPANY agrees, however, to reimburse CONSULTANT for all reasonable and necessary travel and material expenses previously approved in writing by COMPANY.

C. In the event that CONSULTANT completes its work on Game to the sole and complete satisfaction of COMPANY and provides COMPANY with a fully operational prototype thereof on or before **[date]**, COMPANY agrees to pay CONSULTANT a bonus in the amount of **[amount]** U.S. Dollars ($___) ("Bonus"), which shall be due and payable within **[number]** days after submission of and acceptance by COMPANY of the final prototype and documentation for Game. Bonus shall be separate from and in addition to the Consulting Fee. In the event that CONSULTANT fails to complete its work to the complete satisfaction of COMPANY by the aforementioned date, CONSULTANT hereby forfeits any entitlement to this Bonus.

5. CONFIDENTIAL INFORMATION

A. CONSULTANT recognizes that during the course of its retention during the Consulting Term, it may have occasion to review and receive confidential or proprietary information or material from COMPANY including information relating to inventions, patent, trademark and copyright applications, improvements, know-how, specifications, drawings, cost and pricing data, process flow diagrams, bills, customer and vendor lists, ideas, and/or any other written material referring to same ("Confidential Information").

B. CONSULTANT covenants and agrees that both during and after termination of this Agreement, it and its employees, affiliates, and subsidiaries will retain such Confidential Information in confidence pursuant to the following terms and conditions:

1. CONSULTANT agrees to maintain in confidence any such Confidential Information disclosed by COM-

PANY relating to the Field that was not previously known to CONSULTANT or to the general public, or that was not in the public domain prior to such disclosure.

2. Such Confidential Information shall be maintained in confidence by CONSULTANT unless or until:

(a) It shall have been made public by an act or omission of a party other than CONSULTANT;

(b) CONSULTANT receives such Confidential Information from an unrelated third party on a non-confidential basis; or

(c) The passage of **[number]** years from the date of disclosure, whichever shall first occur.

3. Upon request, CONSULTANT agrees to promptly return to COMPANY any materials obtained from or through COMPANY, including all memoranda, drawings, patent, trademark and copyright applications, specifications, and process or flow diagrams including any copies, notes, or memoranda made by CONSULTANT that, in any way, relate to Field or Confidential Information disclosed or transmitted to CONSULTANT by COMPANY.

4. CONSULTANT agrees that it will not, without first obtaining the prior written permission of COMPANY:

(a) Directly or indirectly utilize such Confidential Information in its business;

(b) Manufacture or sell any product that is based in whole or in part on such Confidential Information; or

(c) Disclose such Confidential Information to any third party.

C. CONSULTANT shall not originate any publicity, news release, or other public announcement, written or oral, relating to this Agreement to any amendment hereto or to performance hereunder, without the prior written approval of COMPANY.

6. NON-COMPETITION

CONSULTANT shall not during the Term of this Agreement render any services, directly or indirectly, to any entity engaged in the creation, design, development, and/or marketing of video games. CONSULTANT shall not, for a period of **[number]** year(s) after the termination or expiration of this Agreement, render any services, directly or indirectly, to any entity engaged in the creation, design, development, and/or marketing of video games utilizing technology of the type licensed by **[patent owner]** to COMPANY for Game.

7. INVENTIONS

A. Any inventions, improvements, concepts, or ideas made or conceived by CONSULTANT in connection with and during the performance of services hereunder and related to the business of COMPANY and for **[number]** months thereafter, shall be considered the sole and exclusive property of COMPANY. As part of the services to be performed hereunder, CONSULTANT shall keep written notebook records of its work, properly witnessed for use as invention records, and shall submit such records to COMPANY when requested or at the termination of CONSULTANT's services hereunder. CONSULTANT shall not reproduce any portion of such notebook records without the prior express written consent of COMPANY. CONSULTANT shall promptly and fully report all such inventions to COMPANY.

B. Any work performed by CONSULTANT under this Agreement shall be considered a "Work Made for Hire" as that phrase is defined by the U.S. copyright laws and shall be owned by and for the express benefit of COMPANY. In the event it should be established that such work does not qualify as a Work Made for Hire, CONSULTANT agrees to and does hereby assign to COMPANY all of its right, title, and interest in such work product including, but not limited to, all copyrights, patents, trademarks, and other proprietary rights.

C. Both during the Term of this Agreement and thereafter, CONSULTANT shall fully cooperate with COMPANY in the protection and enforcement of any intellectual property rights that may derive as a result of the services performed by CONSULTANT under the terms of this Agreement. This shall include executing, acknowledging, and delivering to COMPANY all documents or papers that may be necessary to enable COMPANY to publish or protect said inventions, improvements, and ideas.

8. TERMINATION

A. Either party may terminate this Agreement on **[number]** days' written notice to the other party in the event of a breach of any material provision of this

Agreement by the other party, provided that, during the **[number]**-day period, the breaching party fails to cure such breach or, should the breach not be curable within said **[number]**-day period, the breaching party has not initiated steps to cure such breach.

B. Either party shall have the right to terminate this Agreement for any reason and at any time on **[number]** days' written notice to the other party, such termination to become effective at the conclusion of such **[number]**-day period.

C. In the event of a termination or expiration of this Agreement, all covenants and obligations of the parties shall expressly survive termination.

D. COMPANY shall have the right to immediately terminate this Agreement in the event of disability or death to the Lead Consultant or in the event that the Lead Consultant should no longer be employed by CONSULTANT.

9. NOTICES
A. Any notice required to be given pursuant to this Agreement shall be in writing and mailed by certified or registered mail, return receipt requested, or delivered by a national overnight express service such as Federal Express, or by telefax communication with an acknowledgment by the recipient.

B. Either party may change the address to which notice or payment is to be made by written notice to the other party under any provision of this Paragraph.

10. JURISDICTION AND DISPUTES

A. This Agreement shall be governed by the laws of **[state]**.

B. All disputes hereunder shall be resolved in the applicable state or federal courts of **[state]**. The parties consent to the jurisdiction of such courts, agree to accept service of process by mail, and waive any jurisdictional or venue defenses otherwise available.

11. AGREEMENT BINDING ON SUCCESSORS

This Agreement shall be binding on and shall inure to the benefit of the parties hereto, and their heirs, administrators, successors, and assigns.

12. WAIVER

No waiver by either party of any default shall be deemed as a waiver of any prior or subsequent default of the same or other provisions of this Agreement.

13. SEVERABILITY

If any provision hereof is held invalid or unenforceable by a court of competent jurisdiction, such invalidity shall not affect the validity or operation of any other provision, and such invalid provision shall be deemed to be severed from the Agreement.

14. ASSIGNABILITY

This Agreement and the rights and obligations hereunder are personal with respect to CONSULTANT and may not be assigned by any act of CONSULTANT or by operation of law. COMPANY shall, however, have the absolute unfettered right to assign this Agreement and the rights and obligations hereunder to the successor in interest to COMPANY or to the purchaser of any of the assets of COMPANY.

15. INTEGRATION

This Agreement constitutes the entire understanding of the parties, and revokes and supersedes all prior agreements between the parties and is intended as a final expression of their Agreement. It shall not be modified or amended except in writing signed by the parties hereto and specifically referring to this Agreement. This Agreement shall take precedence over any other documents that may be in conflict therewith.

IN WITNESS WHEREOF, the parties hereto, intending to be legally bound hereby, have each caused to be affixed hereto its or his/her hand and seal the day indicated.

[name of COMPANY]   **[name of CONSULTANT]**

By: _____   By: _____
Title: _____   Title: _____
Date: _____   Date: _____

APPENDIX FIVE:
Sample Option Agreement

DATE: **[date]**

For the below stated, non-refundable, option payment, receipt of which is hereby acknowledged, and subject to the following terms, **[name of Inventor]**, a **[state]** corporation with offices at **[address]** ("INVENTOR") hereby grants **[name of company]**, a **[state]** corporation with offices at **[address]** ("COMPANY") an option to further evaluate the following product concepts (the "Products"):

Product Concept Name	**Option Payment**
[name]	**[amount of option]**
[name]	**[amount of option]**
Total Option Payment:	**[total amount]**

1. The option will expire in 60 (sixty) days from the above date.

2. During the option period, INVENTOR will not show the Products to any other party.

3. COMPANY may exercise its option by:

(a) notifying INVENTOR in writing of such intention prior to expiration of the option period; and

(b) simultaneously paying INVENTOR a non-refundable fee in the amount of **[amount]** ($____) per Product.

4. Thereupon, INVENTOR and COMPANY shall enter into a formal license agreement within **[number]** days. The advance on royalties in the license agreement shall be no less than **[number]** Percent (__%) of the option payment and the royalty rate shall be **[number]** Percent (___%). All monies paid by COMPANY in connection with the option shall be credited, on a concept by concept basis, against such advances on royalties.

5. In the event that COMPANY does not exercise its option or enter into a license agreement with INVENTOR, all rights in the product concept shall revert to INVENTOR who shall be free to commercialize the product concept. Further, in such event, COMPANY shall:

(a) turn over to INVENTOR all materials relating to the product concept including materials generated by COMPANY; and

(b) not use or disclose to any third party information relating to the Products.

[name of INVENTOR]   **[name of COMPANY]**

By: ─────────────   By: ─────────────
Title: ───────────   Title: ───────────
Date: ───────────   Date: ───────────

Appendix Six:
Sample Patent License Agreement with Annotations

This Agreement is entered into this **[date]** by and between **[name of LICENSOR]**, a **[country]** citizen, whose address is **[address]** ("LICENSOR"), and **[name of LICENSEE]**, a **[type of organization]**, with offices at **[address]** ("LICENSEE").

> *This is considered part of the preamble to the agreement and is used to identify the relevant parties and their addresses. Care should be taken to insure that the contracting parties are truly the ones with whom you are dealing and not divisions. The attorney should insure that the inventive entity is the one that actually owns rights in the particular patent.*

WITNESSETH:

WHEREAS, LICENSOR is the sole and exclusive owner of Letters Patents of the U.S. No. **[number]**, entitled **[name]**, issued **[date]** ("'000 Patent") and No. **[number]**, entitled **[name]**, issued **[date]** ("'001 Patent") (collectively, "Licensed Patents"); and

WHEREAS, LICENSEE desires to acquire a non-exclusive and nontransferable license under the Licensed Patents for use in the development and sale of

221

the types of products ("Licensed Products") listed in Schedule "A," attached hereto; and

WHEREAS, LICENSOR has the power and authority to grant to LICENSEE such license.

> *Most attorneys use the whereas clauses to "set the stage" for the agreement, i.e., stating what each of the parties brings to the table and what the parties intend to accomplish by entering into the agreement.*
> *While such provisions are of little probative value in most United States courts, many foreign courts place a great deal of emphasis on the intentions of the contracting parties as recited in these clauses. Accordingly, if the agreement may potentially have to be construed by a court outside the United States, particular attention should be paid to these recitations.*
> *Note the identification in these clauses of the patents that will be the subject of this agreement as well as the types of licensed products.*

NOW, THEREFORE, in consideration of the premises and the mutual covenants of this Agreement, the parties hereto agree as follows:

1. LICENSE

A. LICENSOR hereby grants to LICENSEE, upon and subject to all the terms and conditions of this Agreement, a nonexclusive license under the Licensed Patents to make, use, and sell apparatus embodying the inventions described in the Licensed Patents, for the life of such Licensed Patents, in any and all countries, territories, and possessions where the Licensed Patents are effective.

The patent grant gives the licensee authorization to "make, use and sell" and, accordingly, the language of the license agreement conforms to the patent grant. Note that the territory is simply the country or countries where the licensor has patent protection. Thus, if there is no patent protection in a particular country, that country is not included in the licensed territory. The licensee may still practice the invention in that country, however, with no royalty obligation to the licensor.
The grant of nonexclusive licenses is quite common in the patent area, much more so than in trademark and copyright licensing. This, of course, preserves for the patent owner the ability to grant other nonexclusive licenses. From the perspective of the licensee, there may be some advantages to seeking an exclusive license, i.e., to prevent competitors from utilizing the patent.

B. As used in the Agreement, the Licensed Patents shall mean and include:

1. U.S. Patent No. **[number]** entitled **[name]**, issued **[date]**, and No. **[number]** entitled **[name]**, issued **[date]**, and patents on improvements thereof;

2. Any divisional, continuation, or substitute U.S. patent application that shall be based on U.S. Patent Nos. **[number]** and **[number]**;

3. Any patents that shall issue on any of the above-described patent applications or on any improvements thereof, and any reissues and extensions thereof;

4. Patents and patent applications corresponding to each of the above-described patents and patent applications that are issued, filed, or to be filed in any

and all foreign countries; any patents (including but not limited to patents of importation, improvement, or addition, utility models, and inventors certificates) that shall subsequently issue thereof; and

    5. any renewals, divisions, reissues, continuations, or extensions thereof.

> *This provision identifies the specific patents that are to be included in the agreement. It also identifies the related applications that are similarly covered, i.e., continuations, divisions, etc. These patents, upon issuance, become part of the agreement.*

    C. In the event that LICENSEE wishes that a corresponding patent application of any other country, territory, or possession be filed, it shall notify LICENSOR of that wish, and LICENSOR shall thereupon promptly notify LICENSEE whether it will file such other patent application. Failing such agreement, LICENSOR shall at LICENSEE's notification, permit LICENSEE to file such patent application and prosecute it to issuance or final rejection; all cost and expense incurred by LICENSEE, however, shall be deductible from royalties. Such patent application, any patent issuing thereon, and any renewals and extensions thereof shall be added to the aforesaid Licensed Patents, and LICENSOR shall have the title thereto.

> *There may be occasions where the licensee will want patent protection in a country where the licensor had not heretofore filed for such protection. This would invariably be to prevent a competitor from entering that market since the licensee is otherwise free to market the licensed products into*

that country without incurring a royalty obligation. Under this provision, the licensee would request that the licensor seek patent protection in such country at the licensee's expense.

Practically speaking, such a provision is only effective in the early stages of the patent when it still might be possible for the patent owner to file foreign applications and receive convention priorities, e.g., usually within the first year of the filing of the home country application.

D. With the exception of patent applications filed by LICENSEE pursuant to Subparagraph 1.C above, all patent applications comprised within the Licensed Patents shall be prosecuted to issuance or final rejection by LICENSOR at its own cost and expense. Any taxes, annuities, working fees, maintenance fees, and/or renewal and extension charges with respect to each patent application and patent subject to this Agreement shall be punctually paid by LICENSOR.

It is a fundamental precept of patent licensing that the licensor bears the cost of obtaining and maintaining the patents. That is, after all, what the licensee is paying a royalty on.

2. RESERVATION

The license granted in Paragraph 1 of this Agreement is subject to a reserved, nonexclusive, non-assignable license in LICENSOR to make, use, and sell apparatus embodying the invention of the Licensed Patents. LICENSEE may not grant sublicenses under this agreement with the following exception: **[company name and business formation, e.g., an Illinois corporation]** with offices at **[address]**.

While the license grant is a nonexclusive license that is "non-transferable," the agreement expressly

225

prohibits the licensee from granting sublicenses to any party other than a specifically enumerated party.

The licensee may seek greater flexibility in granting sublicenses or, at the very least, the ability to grant sublicenses with the licensor's consent, which consent shall not be unreasonably withheld.

3. TERM

This Agreement shall be effective as of the date of execution by both parties and shall expire simultaneously with the expiration of the longest-lived patent or the rejection or abandonment beyond further appeal of the last-remaining patent application comprised within the Licensed Patents, whichever occurs later, unless sooner terminated by the parties pursuant to the terms of this Agreement (the "Term").

Care must be taken with respect to the term of patent license agreements as the term may never extend beyond the life of the last-to-expire patent. Similarly, consideration should be given to the term of a license where the underlying property rights are patent applications. In the event that a patent never issues, the licensee does not want to have to continue to pay royalties for what amounts to no protection. As such, the licensee should seek to have the agreement terminate upon a final rejection or abandonment of the patent application.

4. COMPENSATION

A. In consideration for the licenses granted hereunder, LICENSEE agrees to pay to LICENSOR the royalty recited in Schedule A ("Royalty") based on LICENSEE's Net Sales of Licensed Products up to the total but not in excess of the amount recited in Schedule A ("Total Royalty") where such Licensed Products are covered by a subsisting and unexpired claim, in the country in which the Licensed Product is manufactured or sold, of any patent of that country comprised within the Licensed Patents. From and after the payment of the Total Royalty by LICENSEE, LICENSEE shall have thereafter a paid-up, royalty-free license to make, have made, use, and sell the Licensed Products.

> *Under this provision, the parties have negotiated an ongoing royalty up to a maximum amount. When the royalty reaches that maximum amount, the license is deemed paid-up and the licensee may continue to practice the invention without incurring any further royalty obligation. There are as many royalty formulae as there are attorneys drafting license agreements. These range from ongoing royalties of a stated percent or stated dollar value per item to a paid up license. Clearly, the attorneys will have to choose the compensation provisions that suits the particular deal. In the multimedia area, the attorney must always consider the fact that there will be multiple royalties for the product and, as such, attempt to minimize the individual royalties wherever possible.*

B. Only one royalty shall be paid hereunder as to Licensed Product whether or not it is covered by more than one (1) claim of a patent, by the claims of more than one (1) patent, or by the claims of patents of more than one (1) country.

> *What the parties intended by this provision is to avoid any possible confusion that multiple patents could result in multiple royalties. The subject license is a "package" license for multiple patents and only one royalty obligation should accrue.*

C. Should LICENSEE grant any sublicenses, the terms and conditions of such sublicenses and the identity of sublicensees shall rest in LICENSEE's discretion, provided that they shall be co-terminated with this Agreement and in accordance with paragraph 2, above. LICENSEE shall pay to LICENSOR, with the royalties to be paid to LICENSOR with respect to LICENSEE's own sales under this Agreement, a royalty based on its sublicensee's activities at the same rate, calculated upon the same definition of Net Sales Price to be reported upon and subject to audit, and payable at the same time as stipulated herein as to LICENSEE's own acts.

> *This sublicensing provision imposes on the licensee an obligation to virtually "pass along" the sublicensee's royalty to the licensor unless it is able to obtain a higher royalty from the sublicensee. In the event that the sublicensee's royalty rate is lower, there is seemingly an obligation on the part of the licensee to supplement the sublicensee's royalty. The provision also requires that the sublicense agreement not extend beyond the term of the license agreement.*
>
> *It might be easier for the parties to agree to a "split" of the sublicensing income on some equitable sharing, e.g., 50/50, 70/30, etc. Such provision would encourage the sublicensing activity.*

D. The Royalty owed LICENSOR shall be calculated on a semiannual calendar basis ("Royalty Period") and shall be payable no later than **[number]** days after the termination of the preceding full semiannual period, i.e., commencing on the first (1st) day of January and July, except that the first and last calendar periods may be "short," depending on the effective date of this Agreement.

Semiannual and quarterly reporting is the norm in the licensing industry with royalty statements due thirty days after close of the royalty period. Many companies will want to extend this period to a 60-day reporting period, particularly where international sales are included.

E. For each Royalty Period, LICENSEE shall provide LICENSOR with a written royalty statement in a form acceptable to LICENSOR. Such royalty statement shall be certified as accurate by a duly authorized officer of LICENSEE reciting, on a country-by-country basis, the stock number, item, units sold, description, quantity shipped, gross invoice, amount billed customers less discounts, allowances, returns, and reportable sales for each Licensed Product. Such statements shall be furnished to LICENSOR regardless of whether any Licensed Products were sold during the Royalty Period or whether any actual Royalty was owed.

The specificity of the royalty statements is important as it will be the document used by a royalty investigator in conducting the audit of the licensee.

F. LICENSEE agrees to pay to LICENSOR an Advance against Royalties in the amount recited in Schedule A, which may be credited against LICENSEE's actual royalty obligation to LICENSOR.

The advance is the payment made by the licensee upon execution of the agreement for which a credit may be taken against its earned royalty obligation. The range of advances can range from nothing to millions of dollars, depending upon the property involved.

G. "Net Sales" shall mean LICENSEE's gross sales (the gross invoice amount billed customers) of Licensed Products, less excise taxes, discounts, and allowances actually shown on the invoice (except cash discounts that are not deductible in the calculation of Royalty) and, further, less any *bona fide* returns (net of all returns actually made or allowed as supported by credit memoranda actually issued to the customers) up to the amount of the actual sales of the Licensed Products during the Royalty Period. No other costs incurred in the manufacturing, selling, advertising, and distribution of the Licensed Products shall be deducted nor shall any deduction be allowed for any uncollectible accounts or allowances.

> *The definition of "net sales" serves to define the royalty base on which the royalty is calculated by multiplying the royalty base by the royalty rate recited above.*
>
> *There are ways to increase a licensor's total compensation from a license agreement without raising the royalty rate. While there is little question that a two point increase in the royalty rate can bring increased revenues to the licensor, it will almost certainly evoke a protest from the licensee. An experienced licensing attorney, however, may be able to achieve the same net result by simply fine tuning the definition of net sales to thereby increase the royalty base on which the total royalty is calculated, thus sidestepping the licensee's wrath.*

H. A Royalty obligation shall accrue upon the sale of the Licensed Products regardless of the time of collection by LICENSEE. A Licensed Product shall be considered "sold" when such Licensed Product is billed, invoiced, shipped, or paid for, whichever occurs first.

This provision is directed to consignment sales where the royalty obligation would be deferred until such time as the money was actually received by the licensee. Under this provision, the royalty obligation would commence at the earliest of the enumerated events rather than upon payment.

I. If LICENSEE sells any Licensed Products to any affiliated or related party at a price less than the regular price charged to other parties, the Royalty shall be computed at the regular price.

A concern of many property owners/licensors is that the licensee will sell licensed products to a related company at a reduced or "favored" price and use that lower price as the royalty base price. In such event, this provision would require an adjustment of that favored price to the regular price to unrelated third parties.

J. The receipt or acceptance by LICENSOR of any royalty statement or payment shall not prevent LICENSOR from subsequently challenging the validity or accuracy of such statement or payment.

The intention of this provision is to avoid an "estoppel"-type argument that once the licensor accepts the royalty statement it is precluded or estopped from subsequently challenging it. In actuality, the acceptance of such a royalty statement should never preclude a subsequent challenge which is frequently based on a royalty investigation or audit.

K. Upon expiration or termination of this Agreement, all Royalty obligations, including the Guaranteed Minimum Royalty, shall be accelerated and shall immediately become due and payable.

> *This is known as an "acceleration" provision intended to accelerate the date when moneys are otherwise due. Absent such a provision, a property owner might have to wait months (or even years) for guaranteed minimum royalties to become due. Under such a provision, when the agreement terminates, all future guaranteed payments immediately become due and payable.*
> *This provision may be limited to terminations for reasons other than a breach of the agreement by the licensor as it might be unfair to require acceleration where the termination was due to a breach by the licensor.*

L. All payments due LICENSOR shall be made in United States currency by check drawn on a U.S. bank, unless otherwise specified by LICENSOR.

> *This provision is intended to cover the sell-off provisions provided for in the agreement, i.e., where the licensee can continue to sell inventory after termination of the agreement. Under the provision, the parties recognize that such sales remain royalty bearing sales.*

M. All payments due LICENSOR based on sales in countries outside the United States shall accrue in the currency of the country in which the sales are made. LICENSEE shall utilize its best efforts to effect U.S. dollar transfers with respect to such Royalties. However, any and all loss of exchange value, taxes, or other expenses incurred in the transfer or conversion of foreign currency into U.S. dollars, and any income, remittance, or other taxes on such Royalties required to be withheld at the source shall be the exclusive responsibility of LICENSOR.

N. In the event that currency regulations of a country in which sales are made prohibit the deposit or payment of royalties to LICENSOR or its nominee, no royalty payment shall accrue or be due and payable by LICENSEE with respect to such sales for so long as such restrictions prevail.

> *This is known as a "blocked currency" provision that relieves the licensee of having to pay royalties where it has not received the income from the sale of the product on which to pay the royalty. It is particularly useful when the license agreement is worldwide with anticipated sales in Eastern Europe, India and South America.*
> *This is an excellent provision to include in all license agreements, particularly where the agreement includes countries with currency restrictions.*

O. Late payments shall incur interest at the rate of **[number]** Percent (___%) per month from the date such payments were originally due.

> *This is a classic interest provision. A simple one percent per month is used, although the fixed fee can rise or fall in accordance with the prevailing interest rates.*
> *In times where there may be fluctuations in rates, it may be advisable to fix the interest rate on the prevailing prime rate (i.e., two points above the then prevailing prime rate). In such instances, it is advisable to establish whose prime rate will be used and as of what date. There should be some consideration to usury laws in different states to insure that the interest provision does not exceed such laws.*

5. RECORD INSPECTION AND AUDIT

A. LICENSOR shall have the right, upon reasonable notice, to inspect LICENSEE's books and records and all other documents and material in LICENSEE's possession or control with respect to the subject matter of this Agreement. LICENSOR shall have free and full access thereto for such purposes and may make copies thereof. In no event shall LICENSOR have the right to examine information with respect to LICENSEE's costs, pricing formulas, or percentages of markup. LICENSEE shall impose similar obligations on its sublicensees for the benefit of itself and of LICENSOR.

> *Most property owners will want the right to inspect the books and records of their licensees to insure that they have been properly paid. The ability to make copies of the inspected records is quite important and should not be overlooked.*
>
> *A licensee might want to restrict the inspection to one conducted by a certified public accountant or accounting professional to insure that it is not the licensor's brother who conducts the audit. Similarly, licensees might want to limit the number of times that an audit can be conducted in any year (no more than once) as well as the minimum amount of notice that must be given (i.e., at least five business days).*
>
> *Note that this provision expressly prohibits the licensor from being able to examine pricing and mark-up data as this does not go toward the calculation of the royalty owed the licensee.*

B. In the event that such inspection reveals an underpayment by LICENSEE of the actual Royalty owed LICENSOR, LICENSEE shall pay the difference, plus interest calculated at the rate of **[number]** Percent (___%) per month. If such underpayment be in excess of **[number]** Dollars ($ _____) for any Royalty Period, LICENSEE shall also reimburse LICENSOR for the cost of such inspection.

> *Pursuant to this provision, in the event that an underpayment is found, the licensee may be obligated to pay for the cost of the inspection. Obviously, this is intended to shift the financial burden for such an inspection to the licensee who was found wanting.*
> *$1,000 may be too low in many circumstances (e.g., where the royalty stream is in the hundreds of thousands of dollars). It may therefore be advisable to set the threshold amount as a percentage of the moneys actually paid (not owed which would be higher). A typical percentage of underpayment is between three and five percent.*

C. All books and records relative to LICENSEE's obligations hereunder shall be maintained and made accessible to LICENSOR for inspection at a location in the United States for at least **[number]** years after termination of this Agreement.

> *Preservation of financial and manufacturing records for a prolonged period of time is critical if one is to conduct a meaningful investigation.*

6. WARRANTIES AND OBLIGATIONS

A. LICENSOR represents and warrants that it is the owner of the entire right, title, and interest in and to the Licensed Patents; that it has the right and power to grant the licenses granted herein; that there are no other agreements with any other party in conflict with such grant; and that it knows of no prior art that would invalidate the Licensed Patents.

> *This warranty is of particular importance in this instance as the licensee will have to rely on such warranty to insure that it is not sued by a third party claiming that it had previously acquired rights in the property from the licensor.*
> *Note the provision concerning knowledge of relevant prior art. Since such art would potentially invalidate the licensed patents, it is imperative that such information (if its exists) be disclosed to the PTO. A licensee will not want to find itself in a situation where it is having to pay a royalty to use a patent which is invalid and the licensor knew of the basis for invalidity.*

B. LICENSOR further represents and warrants that LICENSEE's contemplated use of the Licensed Patents as represented to LICENSOR does not infringe any valid rights of any third party, and that there are no actions for infringement against LICENSOR with respect to items it manufactures and sells embodying the invention of the Licensed Patents anywhere in the world.

> *This is an absolute warranty of non-infringement. Many licensees believe that it is absolutely essential that the licensor be prepared to give such an unconditional warranty.*
> *Licensors may feel more comfortable with a more limited representation and warranty, i.e., that they have no actual knowledge of any such infringement.*

C. LICENSEE shall be solely responsible for the manufacture, production, sale, and distribution of the

Licensed Products and will bear all costs associated therewith.

> *There is little doubt that the licensee should be responsible for all of these costs and expenses. However, where the relationship moves from classic licensor/licensee to joint venture, there may be some degree of sharing of these costs.*

D. In the event that LICENSOR shall develop any improvement to the apparatus claimed in the Licensed Patents, and later incorporated in an improved or modified product by LICENSEE, such improved product shall be subject to the payment of a Royalty. All improvement made by the LICENSEE shall be promptly disclosed to LICENSOR and shall hereinafter become the property of LICENSOR. LICENSEE hereby agrees to execute any and all documents necessary to perfect LICENSOR's rights in such improvements.

> *The first portion of this provision is intended to protect the licensee by providing that should the licensor develop any improvements, such improvements shall be added to the agreement. What the first part gives, however, the second takes away. Under the second part of this provision, should the licensee develop any improvements, they become the property of the licensor. This is referred to as a "grant back" provision.*
> *Universally, licensees rebel at the inclusion of grant back provisions in license agreements. Such rebellion is for obvious reasons. Unless absolutely necessary, a licensee should not consider agreeing to such a provision.*

7. MARKING AND SAMPLES

A. LICENSEE shall, and agrees to require its sublicensees to, fully comply with the patent marking provisions of the intellectual property laws of the applicable countries in the Licensed Territory.

It must be appreciated that the property is typically the subject of some intellectual property protection and that in order to maintain such rights, the eventual licensed product must carry appropriate patent, trademark and/or copyright legends. See 35 U.S.C. § 287 for the provisions concerning patent marking; 17 U.S.C. § 401 for the appropriate copyright notice; and 15 U.S.C. § 1111 for the trademark notice requirements.

B. At least once during each calendar year, LICENSEE shall submit to LICENSOR **[number]** samples of each of the Licensed Products.

In order to have a meaningful quality control provision, the licensee must be obligated to submit samples of the licensed products for product approval. This is the provision that so obligates the licensee. Note that there are no approval provisions in this agreement as there is no right of approval for quality.

8. TERMINATION

The following termination rights are in addition to the termination rights that may be provided elsewhere in the Agreement:

A. Immediate Right of Termination. LICENSOR shall have the right to immediately terminate this

Agreement by giving written notice to LICENSEE in the event that LICENSEE does any of the following:

1. Fails to obtain or maintain product liability insurance in the amount and of the type provided for herein;

2. Files a petition in bankruptcy or is adjudicated a bankrupt or insolvent, or makes an assignment for the benefit of creditors or an arrangement pursuant to any bankruptcy law, or if the LICENSEE discontinues or dissolves its business or if a receiver is appointed for LICENSEE or for LICENSEE's business and such receiver is not discharged within **[number]** days;

3. Fails to commence the shipment of Licensed Products within **[number]** months from the Effective Date of this Agreement; or

4. Upon the commencement of sale of Licensed Products, fails to sell any Licensed Products for **[number]** or more consecutive Royalty Periods.

> *Termination provisions are the most important provisions in any license agreement as they will be the first paragraphs reviewed by the attorneys when problems develop in the business relationship. This provision is intended to provide the right to immediately terminate the agreement with no notice and cure right to the licensee in the event of certain material breaches on the part of the licensee. Upon the occurrence of any of these events, there is no reason why the licensee should be given an opportunity to cure the breach and the licensor's rights to terminate the agreement should be absolute.*

Note, however, although termination provisions have traditionally included provisions giving a party the right to terminate the agreement in the event of bankruptcy, such provisions are unenforceable under the Bankruptcy Code.

B. **Right to Terminate Upon Notice.** Either party may terminate this Agreement upon **[number]** days' written notice to the other party in the event of a breach of any provision of this Agreement by the other party, provided that, during the **[number]**-day period, the breaching party fails to cure such breach.

This is a classic "termination/cure" provision that is intended to cover many different eventualities that might occur during the term of this agreement. It requires notice by the non-breaching party and a "cure" period after receipt of the notice before termination is effected.
The cure period (e.g., 60 days) is frequently the subject of some negotiation. Some agreements provide for a 30 day cure period, unless the breach involved the payment of moneys in which case, the cure period for such financial breaches is 10 days. In addition, the provision may give the non-breaching party the right to simply initiate steps to effect a cure rather than cure the breach within the cure period.

C. **LICENSEE Right to Terminate.** LICENSEE shall have the right to terminate this Agreement at any time upon **[number]** days' written notice to LICENSOR, such termination to become effective at the conclusion of such **[number]**-day period.

A licensee should have the unilateral right to terminate a license agreement at any time on notice to the licensor. The question is whether the licensee will obligate itself to future guarantees, etc. The answer is typically found in the acceleration provision which requires, upon termination of the agreement, the balance of all moneys to become immediately due and payable.

9. POST-TERMINATION RIGHTS

Upon expiration or termination of this Agreement, LICENSEE shall thereafter immediately, except for reason of termination because of expiration or a declaration of patent invalidity, cease all further use of the Licensed Patents and all rights granted to LICENSEE or its sublicensees under this Agreement shall forthwith terminate and immediately revert to LICENSOR.

After termination or expiration of the agreement, the licensee is no longer a licensee and therefore has no rights under the agreement. As such, any further activities are at its own peril and risk.

The licensee may want to include a provision providing for a "sell-off" of inventory at the time of termination of the agreement. Such a provision would only apply to a termination of the agreement, since the licensee would have the absolute right to sell off product upon expiration of the patents.

10. INFRINGEMENTS

A. LICENSOR agrees to defend the Licensed Patents against infringement by third parties upon notification by LICENSEE to LICENSOR with the request that LICENSOR proceed to take such steps to end such infringement. If LICENSOR does not institute an infringement suit within **[number]** days after LICENSEE's written request that it do so, or should LICENSOR thereafter fail to press such action vigorously, LICENSEE may institute and prosecute such lawsuit in the name of LICENSOR.

As the owner of the property, the licensor should be given the first opportunity to commence an action for infringement and, under the terms of this provision, is given a window of opportunity to bring such an action. In the event that the licensor does not elect to bring such an action, however, the licensee is given the right to bring an action of its own. There may be reasons to shorten this window of opportunity to the licensor in which to bring an action, particularly where preliminary relief may be sought.

B. Any lawsuit shall be prosecuted solely at the expense of the party bringing suit and all sums recovered shall be divided equally between LICENSOR and LICENSEE after deduction of all reasonable expenses and attorney fees. However, should LICENSEE prosecute such action, it shall further be entitled to deduct from royalties all unrecovered costs and legal fees in connection with the action.

Although a seemingly innocuous provision, this paragraph may have great consequences should there be a recovery against an infringer. The absence of such a provision may give a non-participating licensee a potential cause of action to show that the infringement caused it damage.

C. The parties agree to fully cooperate with the other party in the prosecution of any such suit. The party bringing suit shall reimburse the other party for the expenses incurred as a result of such cooperation.

This is the contractual obligation for cooperation. Clearly, it is more important after termination than during the term of the agreement.

11. INDEMNITY

A. LICENSEE agrees to defend, indemnify, and hold LICENSOR, and its officers, directors, agents, and employees, harmless against all costs, expenses, and losses (including reasonable attorney fees and costs) incurred through claims of third parties against LICENSOR based on the manufacture or sale of the Licensed Products including, but not limited to, actions founded on product liability.

A major concern for most intellectual property licensors is the possibility that they can be brought into a product liability action due to the presence of their property. The purpose of this provision is to protect the licensor against such actions and require that the licensee contractually defend and indemnify the licensor from such eventualities.

B. LICENSOR agrees to defend, indemnify, and hold LICENSEE, and its officers, directors, agents, sublicensees, employees, and customers, harmless against all costs, expenses, and losses (including reasonable attorney fees and costs) incurred through claims of third parties against LICENSEE based on a breach by LICENSOR of any representation and warranty made in this Agreement, including but not limited to claims by a third party of infringement based on the manufacture, use, or sale of items embodying the invention of the Licensed Patents.

Without question, this is the most hotly debated provision in any license agreement. Licensees ar-

gue that they want an absolute indemnification for any infringement action involving the property. Licensors argue that it is simply not fair.

The goal of the inventor is to eliminate liability if at all possible, e.g., agree to an indemnity that is based on third party rights of which he or she is aware; cap that indemnity obligation at the total royalty income received from the company; and finally, apply the indemnity only when a court finds that the inventor breached the warranty, thereby avoiding having to fund frivolous lawsuits. In contrast, the company will seek the right to escrow royalty income to the licensor during the pendency of the third party law suit in an attempt to build a "war chest" to fund the lawsuit. A compromise should lie somewhere between the respective positions of the parties.

12. INSURANCE

LICENSEE shall, throughout the Term of the Agreement, obtain and maintain at its own cost and expense from a qualified insurance company licensed to do business in **[state]** and having a Moody's rating of B+ or better, standard Product Liability Insurance naming LICENSOR, and its officers, directors, employees, agents, and shareholders, as an additional insured. Such policy shall provide protection against all claims, demands, and causes of action arising out of any defects or failure to perform, alleged or otherwise, of the Licensed Products or any material used in connection therewith or any use thereof. The amount of coverage shall be as specified in Schedule A attached hereto. The policy shall provide for **[number]** days' notice to LICENSOR from the insurer by registered or certified mail, return receipt requested, in the event of any modification, cancellation, or termination thereof. LICENSEE agrees to furnish LICEN-

SOR a certificate of insurance evidencing same within **[number]** days after execution of this Agreement and, in no event, shall LICENSEE manufacture, distribute, or sell the Licensed Products prior to receipt by LICENSOR of such evidence of insurance.

> *The product liability insurance provision is intended to support the licensee's indemnity obligation. It is particularly important with smaller licensees. Product liability insurance must be in place prior to any sales of the licensed products to insure that all such sales are covered. Particular care should be exercised relative to the choice of carrier and the amount of the deductible. Insurance carriers have been known to go out of business or go bankrupt. Accordingly, the agreement should provide that the carrier selected have a Moody's Rating of B+ or better (A is even better).*

13. NOTICES

A. Any notice required to be given pursuant to this Agreement shall be in writing and mailed by certified or registered mail, return receipt requested, or delivered by a national overnight express service.

> *This provision identifies the manner in which notices under the agreement must be given. It requires some form of receipt to document that notice was sent. Telefaxing notices is becoming a common way to provide instant receipt, although acknowledgment can be difficult.*

B. Either party may change the address to which notice or payment is to be sent by written notice to the other party pursuant to the provisions of this paragraph.

> *This provision is intended to give both parties the opportunity to change their respective addresses.*

14. JURISDICTION AND DISPUTES

A. This Agreement shall be governed by the laws of **[state]**.

> *Choice of law and choice of forum provisions are two of the most hotly negotiated provisions in any agreement. Care should be taken to understand the distinction between choice of law and choice of forum. Courts will normally defer to the choice of law that the parties have agreed to, if its application is not unreasonable, and the agreement was negotiated freely and voluntarily.*
>
> *A frequently negotiated compromise to the stalemate that may develop when negotiating this provision is to provide that the law of a particular neutral state with a well-developed body of law will govern. Many agreements provide for New York or California law to govern, as both states have a plethora of decisions on most issues which may be relied upon by the parties.*

B. All disputes hereunder shall be resolved in the applicable state or federal courts of **[state]**. The parties consent to the jurisdiction of such courts, agree to accept service of process by mail, and waive any jurisdictional or venue defenses otherwise available.

> *The age-old question of litigation versus arbitration is always a matter of personal preference, typically gleaned from years of personal experience and success. Where a stalemate develops concerning the appropriate forum for dispute resolution, the parties may want to consider a "home and home" provision in which each party agrees to commence the action against the other party in the forum of the other party.*
>
> *When designating a choice of forum provision, it might be wise to designate that the forum has the "exclusive" power to hear such actions. In the ab-*

sence of such an explicit statement, the argument can be made that any jurisdiction having proper jurisdiction and venue can hear the matter.

15. AGREEMENT BINDING ON SUCCESSORS

This Agreement shall be binding on and shall inure to the benefit of the parties hereto, and their heirs, administrators, successors, and assigns.

This is a standard provision which is included in most agreements to protect successor entities and their estates.

16. WAIVER

No waiver by either party of any default shall be deemed as a waiver of any prior or subsequent default of the same or other provisions of this Agreement.

Breaches are frequently ignored or "waived" by both parties. This provision is intended to protect parties to an agreement from permanent modification of the terms of the agreement when one party fails to perform and the other party accepts such non-performance without exercising whatever rights it may have against the non-performing party.

17. SEVERABILITY

If any provision hereof is held invalid or unenforceable by a court of competent jurisdiction, such invalidity shall not affect the validity or operation of any other provision and such invalid provision shall be deemed to be severed from the Agreement.

Severability provisions are meant to cut out a particular provision from the agreement in the event that it is found to be invalid or unenforceable. While courts will typically enforce the balance of an agreement that contains an illegal or otherwise unenforceable provision, such a provision eliminates any argument to the effect that the one invalid provision voids the entire agreement. This is particularly important when a party recognizes that a certain provision (e.g., a non-compete provision) is of questionable enforceability and may be subsequently challenged.

18. ASSIGNABILITY

The license granted hereunder is personal to LICENSEE and may not be assigned by any act of LICENSEE or by operation of law unless in connection with a transfer of substantially all the assets of LICENSEE or with the consent of LICENSOR.

It should be appreciated that agreements and the rights and obligations provided for therein are freely assignable by either party in the absence of a provision prohibiting such transfer. Thus, if the parties intend to limit or restrict the rights of one or both parties to assign an agreement or the underlying rights and obligations, the agreement must specifically contain such a restriction or prohibition.

19. INTEGRATION

This Agreement constitutes the entire understanding of the parties, and revokes and supersedes all prior agreements between the parties and is intended as a final expression of their Agreement. It shall not be modified or amended except in writing signed by the parties hereto and specifically referring to this Agreement. This Agreement shall take precedence over any other documents that may be in conflict therewith.

An integration clause is a contractual provision reciting the intention of the parties that the written contract purports to be the final and complete expression of all terms agreed upon. Integration provisions also define how changes can be made to the agreement in the future. They must be in writing and signed by the parties. As such, oral modifications to the agreement cannot be relied upon in a subsequent litigation.

IN WITNESS WHEREOF, the parties hereto, intending to be legally bound hereby, have each caused to be affixed hereto its or his/her hand and seal the day indicated.

[name of LICENSOR]   **[name of LICENSEE]**

By: ─────────────   By: ─────────────
Title: ───────────   Title: ───────────
Date: ───────────   Date: ───────────

Schedule A

1. Licensed Products

The Licensed Products are as follows:

[Specify licensed products, e.g., CD-ROMs, computer software and all other configurations for all digital/electronic technology systems, whether now known or hereinafter developed, including, but not limited to other computer disk formats

whether sold individually or through transmission to personal computer or other telecommunicated use for interactive television or other home use.]

This is a clear definition of the types of products for which the licensee has been licensed. Often, the license grant will be for any product that is covered by the claims of the patent in question. Most patents are "product" or "use" specific.

2. Royalty Rate

The Royalty Rate is as follows: **[number]** Percent (___%) until such time as the **[patent number]** Patent expires, at which time the Royalty Rate shall decrease to **[number]** Percent (___%).

This royalty rate must be read in conjunction with the total royalty recited below. The parties must come to some equitable compromise as to structuring the royalty compensation.

3. Total Royalty

The Total Maximum Royalty paid by LICENSEE during the Term of this Agreement shall be: **[number]** U.S. Dollars ($___).

This is the maximum compensation that the licensor will receive under the agreement.

4. Advance

The following Advance shall be paid upon execution of this Agreement: **[number]** U.S. Dollars ($___).

The advance is the payment made by the licensee upon execution of the agreement for which a credit may be taken against its earned royalty obligation. The range of advances can range from nothing to millions of dollars, depending upon the property involved.

5. Product Liability Insurance

[Number] Dollars ($___) combined single limit, with a deductible amount not to exceed **[number]** Dollars ($___), for each single occurrence for bodily injury and/or for property damage.

Appendix Seven: Sample Technology License Agreement

This Agreement is entered into this **[date]**, by and **between [name of LICENSOR]**, a **[country]** citizen, whose address is **[address]** ("LICENSOR"), and **[name of LICENSEE]**, a **[type of organization]**, with offices at **[address]** ("LICENSEE").

W I T N E S S E T H:

WHEREAS, LICENSOR is engaged in the business of designing and developing computer-related software and hardware systems and related products and has, over the years, acquired and developed substantial and valuable technical knowledge, know-how and experience in the design and development of such systems and products described in detail in Exhibit A attached hereto (the "Technology"); and

WHEREAS, LICENSEE desires to engage in the business of designing, developing, and selling similar products and utilize the Technology in the design, development, and sale of such products; and

WHEREAS, LICENSOR and LICENSEE believe it is in their mutual interest and desire to enter into an agreement whereby LICENSEE would use LICENSOR's

Technology in the manufacture and sale of the Products in the Territory defined herein below pursuant to the terms and conditions hereinafter provided.

NOW, THEREFORE, in consideration of the premises and the mutual covenants of this Agreement, the parties hereto agree as follows:

1. LICENSE
A. LICENSOR hereby grants to LICENSEE and its sublicensees, for the term of this Agreement, a nonexclusive, non-assignable, right and license to use its Technology in order to manufacture, process, prepare, and sell the products set forth in Schedule A using said Technology (the "Licensed Products") in the countries identified in Schedule A attached hereto (the "Territory"). LICENSEE may grant sublicenses to third parties under the Agreement with the approval of LICENSOR, which approval shall not be unreasonably withheld.

B. No right or license is being conveyed to LICENSEE to export Licensed Products or to otherwise use the Technology in any country other than the Territory.

2. TERM
This Agreement shall be effective as of the date of execution by both parties and shall extend for the period set forth in Schedule A (the "Term").

3. COMPENSATION
A. In consideration for the licenses granted hereunder, LICENSEE agrees to pay to LICENSOR the roy-

alty recited in Schedule A (the "Royalty") based on LICENSEE's Net Sales of Licensed Products.

B. Should LICENSEE grant any sublicenses, LICENSEE shall pay LICENSOR **[number]** Percent (___%) of the total income or compensation received by such sublicensees.

C. The Royalty owed LICENSOR shall be calculated on a semiannual calendar basis ("Royalty Period") and shall be payable no later than **[number]** days after the termination of the preceding full semiannual period, i.e., commencing on the first (1st) day of January and July, except that the first and last calendar periods may be "short," depending on the effective date of this Agreement.

D. For each Royalty Period, LICENSEE shall provide LICENSOR with a written royalty statement in a form acceptable to LICENSOR. Such royalty statement shall be certified as accurate by a duly authorized officer of LICENSEE reciting, on a country-by-country basis, the stock number, item, units sold, description, quantity shipped, gross invoice, amount billed customers less discounts, allowances, returns, and reportable sales for each Licensed Product. Such statements shall be furnished to LICENSOR regardless of whether any Licensed Products were sold during the Royalty Period or whether any actual Royalty was owed.

E. LICENSEE agrees to pay to LICENSOR an Advance against Royalties in the amount recited in Schedule A, which may be credited against LICENSEE's actual royalty obligation to LICENSOR.

F. During each calendar year during the Term of this Agreement, LICENSEE agrees to pay LICENSOR a Guaranteed Minimum Royalty as recited in Schedule A that may be credited against LICENSEE's actual royalty obligation to LICENSOR. The Guaranteed Minimum Royalty shall be calculated at the end of each calendar year. In the event that LICENSEE's actual Royalties paid LICENSOR for any calendar year are less than the Guaranteed Minimum Royalty for such year, LICENSEE shall, in addition to paying LICENSOR its actual earned Royalty for such Royalty Period, pay LICENSOR the difference between the total earned Royalty for the year and the Guaranteed Minimum Royalty for such year.

G. "Net Sales" shall mean LICENSEE's gross sales (the gross invoice amount billed customers) of Licensed Products, less discounts and allowances actually shown on the invoice (except cash discounts that are not deductible in the calculation of Royalty), and, further, less any bona fide returns (net of all returns actually made or allowed as supported by credit memoranda actually issued to the customers) up to the amount of the actual sales of the Licensed Products during the Royalty Period. No other costs incurred in the manufacturing, selling, advertising, and distribution of the Licensed Products shall be deducted nor shall any deduction be allowed for any uncollectible accounts or allowances.

H. A Royalty obligation shall accrue upon the sale of the Licensed Products regardless of the time of collection by LICENSEE. A Licensed Product shall be considered "sold" when such Licensed Product is billed, invoiced, shipped, or paid for, whichever occurs first.

I. If LICENSEE sells any Licensed Products to any affiliated or related party at a price less than the regular price charged to other parties, the Royalty shall be computed at the regular price.

J. The receipt or acceptance by LICENSOR of any royalty statement or payment shall not prevent LICENSOR from subsequently challenging the validity or accuracy of such statement or payment.

K. Upon expiration or termination of this Agreement, all Royalty obligations, including the Guaranteed Minimum Royalty, shall be accelerated and shall immediately become due and payable.

L. LICENSEE's obligations for the payment of Royalties shall survive expiration or termination of this Agreement and will continue for as long as LICENSEE continues to sell the Licensed Products.

M. All payments due LICENSOR shall be made in U.S. currency by check drawn on a U.S. bank, unless otherwise specified by LICENSOR.

N. Late payments shall incur interest at the rate of **[number]** Percent (___%) per month from the date such payments were originally due.

4. RECORD INSPECTION AND AUDIT

A. LICENSOR shall have the right, upon reasonable notice, to inspect LICENSEE's books and records and all other documents and material in LICENSEE's possession or control with respect to the subject matter of this Agreement. LICENSOR shall have free and full access thereto for such purposes and may make copies thereof.

B. In the event that such inspection reveals an underpayment by LICENSEE of the actual Royalty owed LICENSOR, LICENSEE shall pay the difference, plus interest calculated at the rate of **[number]** Percent (__%) per month. If such underpayment be in excess of **[number]** U.S. Dollars ($ ___) for any Royalty Period, LICENSEE shall also reimburse LICENSOR for the cost of such inspection.

C. All books and records relative to LICENSEE's obligations hereunder shall be maintained and made accessible to LICENSOR for inspection at a location in the United States for at least **[number]** years after termination of this Agreement.

5. LICENSOR'S OBLIGATIONS/ CONFIDENTIALITY

A. Beginning upon the effective date of this Agreement as provided in Schedule A, LICENSOR shall meet with and provide LICENSEE with such Technology relating to the installation and operation of hardware, software, machinery, equipment, materials, object codes, specifications, designs, manufacturing and processing procedures, methods, layout, and the like that LICENSOR believes LICENSEE may require in order to manufacture and sell Licensed Products in the Territory.

B. LICENSEE recognizes that such Technology is the proprietary and confidential property of LICENSOR. Accordingly, LICENSEE shall not, without the prior express written consent of LICENSOR, during the term of this Agreement and for **[number]** years thereafter, disclose or reveal to any third party or utilize for its own benefit other than pursuant to this Agreement, any such Technology provided by LICENSOR concerning Products, provided that such information was not previously known to LICENSEE or to the general public. LICENSEE further agrees to take all reasonable precautions to preserve the confidentiality of LICENSOR's Technology and shall assume responsibility that its employees, sublicensees, and assignees will similarly preserve this information against third parties. The provisions of this clause shall survive termination of this Agreement.

C. LICENSOR shall also provide LICENSEE, at its place of manufacture, such technical and other qualified experts for developing the Products and for assisting LICENSEE on any problems or matters that require on-the-spot assistance, and for such periods and in such number as identified in Schedule A annexed hereto. In such event, LICENSEE shall pay all travel and out-of-pocket expenses incurred by any such LICENSOR personnel, it being understood that the salaries of the experts shall be the responsibility of LICENSOR.

D. At the request of LICENSEE, LICENSOR shall train at least **[number]** employees of LICENSEE at LICENSOR's facility. Expenses and salaries of LICENSEE personnel sent to LICENSOR by LICENSEE for training shall be borne by LICENSEE.

E. LICENSOR represents and warrants that it has the right and power to grant the licenses granted herein and that there are no other agreements with any other party in conflict with such grant.

F. LICENSOR further represents and warrants that it has no actual knowledge that the Technology infringes any valid rights of any third party.

6. IMPROVEMENTS

During the term of this Agreement, each party shall advise the other party of any technical improvements and inventions relating to the Technology and the Licensed Products. All such improvements and inventions shall become the property of LICENSOR, and LICENSEE agrees to execute any and all documents requested by LICENSOR in order to perfect LICENSOR's right in same. If such improvement and invention is later incorporated in an improved or modified product by LICENSEE, such improved product shall be subject to the payment of a Royalty. Further, if LICENSEE incorporates any dominant feature of the Property on other products, such other products shall be subject to the payment of a Royalty.

7. MACHINERY

A. Where applicable, at the request of LICENSEE, LICENSOR shall supply and cause to be supplied to LICENSEE such necessary machinery, equipment, and other materials as is available to LICENSOR. Prices of the machinery, equipment, and other materials from and through LICENSOR shall be on most favored terms with those established by or through LICENSOR.

B. Where applicable, LICENSOR will lease the said equipment to LICENSEE for a **[number]**-year period for an annual U.S. dollar amount of **[number]** Dollars ($ ___) per annum. Upon termination of this Agreement, LICENSEE shall return said equipment to LICENSOR at LICENSOR's expense.

8. TECHNICAL INFORMATION

LICENSOR represents that the technical information and assistance relating to the Technology conveyed under this Agreement shall be provided with reasonable care and will, where applicable, be of the same types as currently practiced by LICENSOR.

9. LICENSEE'S OBLIGATIONS

A. LICENSEE represents that it has the financial resources and business operations that will enable it to manufacture, distribute, sell, and otherwise reasonably commercialize the Licensed Products throughout the Territory, and that it shall, during the term of this Agreement and any renewal thereof, use its best efforts to promote the distribution and sale of such Licensed Products in the Territory. LICENSEE further agrees that it will, in good faith and with reasonable diligence, conduct all operations including manufacturing, marketing, distribution, and sale of Licensed Products in accordance with the highest standards of business customs of the industry and that it will endeavor to sell Licensed Products throughout the Territory, utilizing its skill and resources in such effort to the extent that high standards of business practice and judgment dictate.

B. LICENSEE shall fully comply with the marking provisions of the intellectual property laws of the applicable countries in the Licensed Territory.

10. PERMITS

A. In the event that the Technology is to be used in foreign countries by LICENSEE or its sublicensees, this Agreement is subject to the obtaining of all necessary permits required by the laws of that particular country. LICENSEE shall take all steps necessary for obtaining from the appropriate governmental authority all approvals and permits necessary to carry out the terms of this Agreement.

B. LICENSOR shall cooperate with LICENSEE relative to supplying any information and material necessary for the approvals and consents of the appropriate governmental authority.

11. TERMINATION

The following termination rights are in addition to the termination rights which may be provided elsewhere in the Agreement:

A. Immediate Right of Termination. LICENSOR shall have the right to immediately terminate this Agreement by giving written notice to LICENSEE in the event that LICENSEE does any of the following:

1. Fails to obtain or maintain product liability insurance in the amount and of the type provided for herein;

2. Files a petition in bankruptcy or is adjudicated a bankrupt or insolvent, or makes an assignment for

the benefit of creditors or an arrangement pursuant to any bankruptcy law, or if LICENSEE discontinues or dissolves its business or if a receiver is appointed for LICENSEE or for LICENSEE's business and such receiver is not discharged within **[number]** days;

3. Fails to commence the sale of Licensed Products within **[number]** months from the Effective Date of this Agreement; or

4. Upon the commencement of sale of Licensed Products, fails to sell any Licensed Product for **[number]** consecutive Royalty Periods.

B. Right to Terminate Upon Notice. Either party may terminate this Agreement on **[number]** days' written notice to the other party in the event of a breach of any provision of this Agreement by the other party, provided that, during the **[number]**-day period, the breaching party fails to cure such breach.

C. LICENSEE Right to Terminate. LICENSEE shall have the right to terminate this Agreement at any time upon **[number]** months' written notice to LICENSOR for any reason.

12. POST-TERMINATION RIGHTS

A. Upon the expiration or termination of this Agreement, all rights granted to LICENSEE under this Agreement shall forthwith terminate and immediately revert to LICENSOR and LICENSEE shall discontinue all use of the Technology and the like.

B. Upon the expiration or termination of this Agreement, LICENSOR may require that LICENSEE transmit to LICENSOR, at no cost, all material relating to the Technology, provided, however, that LICENSEE shall be permitted to retain a full copy of all material subject to the confidentiality provisions of this agreement.

13. INDEMNITY

A. LICENSEE agrees to defend, indemnify, and hold LICENSOR, and its officers, directors, agents, and employees, harmless against all costs, expenses, and losses (including reasonable attorney fees and costs) incurred through claims of third parties against LICENSOR based on the manufacture or sale of the Licensed Products including, but not limited to, actions founded on product liability.

B. LICENSOR agrees to defend, indemnify, and hold LICENSEE, and its officers, directors, agents, and employees, harmless against all costs, expenses and losses (including reasonable attorney fees and costs) incurred through claims of third parties against LICENSEE based on a breach by LICENSOR of any representation or warranty made in this Agreement.

14. INSURANCE

LICENSEE shall, throughout the Term of the Agreement, obtain and maintain at its own cost and expense from a qualified insurance company licensed to do business in **[state]** and having a Moody's Rating of B+ or better standard Product Liability Insurance naming LICENSOR, and its officers, directors, employees, agents, and shareholders, as an additional insured. Such policy shall provide protection against all claims, demands, and causes of action arising out of any defects or failure to perform, alleged or otherwise, of the Licensed Products or any material used in connection therewith or any use thereof. The amount of coverage shall be as specified in Schedule A attached hereto. The policy shall provide for **[number]** days' notice to LICENSOR from the insurer by registered or certified mail, return receipt requested, in the event of any modification, cancellation, or termination thereof. LICENSEE agrees to furnish LICENSOR a certificate of insurance evidencing same within **[number]** days after execution of this Agreement, if practical, and, in no event, shall LICENSEE manufacture, distribute, or sell the Licensed Products prior to receipt by LICENSOR of such evidence of insurance.

15. NOTICES

A. Any notice required to be given pursuant to this Agreement shall be in writing and mailed by certified or registered mail, return receipt requested, or delivered by a national overnight express service.

B. Either party may change the address to which notice or payment is to be sent by written notice to the other party pursuant to the provisions of this paragraph.

16. JURISDICTION AND DISPUTES

A. This Agreement shall be governed by the laws of **[state]**.

B. All disputes hereunder shall be resolved in the applicable state or federal courts of **[state]**. The parties consent to the jurisdiction of such courts, agree to accept service of process by mail, and waive any jurisdictional or venue defenses otherwise available.

17. AGREEMENT BINDING ON SUCCESSORS

This Agreement shall be binding on and shall inure to the benefit of the parties hereto, and their heirs, administrators, successors, and assigns.

18. WAIVER

No waiver by either party of any default shall be deemed as a waiver of any prior or subsequent default of the same or other provisions of this Agreement.

19. SEVERABILITY

If any provision hereof is held invalid or unenforceable by a court of competent jurisdiction, such invalidity shall not affect the validity or operation of any other provision and such invalid provision shall be deemed to be severed from the Agreement.

20. ASSIGNABILITY

The license granted hereunder is personal to LICENSEE and may not be assigned by any act of LICENSEE or by operation of law unless in connection with a transfer of substantially all the assets of LICENSEE or with the consent of LICENSOR.

21. INTEGRATION

This Agreement constitutes the entire understanding of the parties, and revokes and supersedes all prior agreements between the parties and is intended as a final expression of their Agreement. It shall not be modified or amended except in writing signed by the parties hereto and specifically referring to this Agreement. This Agreement shall take precedence over any other documents that may be in conflict therewith.

IN WITNESS WHEREOF, the parties hereto, intending to be legally bound hereby, have each caused to be affixed hereto its or his/her hand and seal the day indicated.

[name of LICENSOR]   **[name of LICENSEE]**

By: _____   By: _____
Title: _____   Title: _____
Date: _____   Date: _____

SCHEDULE A

1. Licensed Products

The Licensed Products are as follows:

[Specify licensed products, e.g., CD-ROMs, computer software and all other configurations for all digital/electronic technology systems, whether now known or hereinafter developed, including, but not limited to, other computer disk formats whether sold individually or through transmission to personal computers or other telecommunicated use for interactive television or other home use.]

2. Licensed Territory

The following countries shall constitute the Licensed Territory:

[state territory, e.g., United States and Canada].

3. The Term

[Number] years from the effective date thereof, and thereafter, shall be automatically renewable for successive **[number]**-year periods, unless **[number]** days prior to the termination any party hereto gives written notice to the other party of its election not to renew this Agreement for an additional **[number]**-year period, in which event this Agreement shall terminate at the end of the period in which such notice was given.

4. Royalty Rate

The Royalty Rate is as follows: **[number]** Percent (___%).

5. Advance

The following Advance shall be paid upon execution of this Agreement: **[number]** Dollars ($ ___).

6. Product Liability Insurance

[Number] Dollars ($ ___) combined single limit, with a deductible amount not to exceed **[number]** Dollars ($ ___), for each single occurrence for bodily injury and for property damage.

EXHIBIT A

[Attach volume of drawings and other technical information being disclosed by LICENSOR to LICENSEE.]

Appendix Eight:
Sample Multimedia License Agreement

This Agreement is made this **[date]** by and between **[name of OWNER]**, a **[type of organization]** with offices at **[address]** ("OWNER"), and **[name of COMPANY]**, a **[type of organization]** with offices at **[address]** ("COMPANY").

WITNESSETH:

WHEREAS, COMPANY controls all rights with respect to a board game entitled **[name]** ("Property") originally developed by **[name]** ("Developer") pursuant to an agreement entered into between COMPANY and Developer dated **[date]** including, but not limited to, rights with respect to the development of video and multimedia games;

WHEREAS, COMPANY is in the business of creating, developing, and marketing video and multimedia games;

WHEREAS, COMPANY is desirous of obtaining from OWNER the exclusive right and license to develop the Property into an interactive, multimedia video game to be marketed on **[specify type, e.g., CD-ROM]** ("Media") for a **[specify type, e.g., PC]** Platform ("Platform") in the **[specify type, e.g., Windows]** operating system ("Operating System") in the **[specify language, e.g., English]** language ("Language") ("Licensed Products"); and

WHEREAS, COMPANY seeks to develop an ancillary licensing program with respect to the Licensed Product subject to a sharing in the income derived from such ancillary licensing program with OWNER;

NOW, THEREFORE, in consideration of the promises and agreements set forth herein, the parties, each intending to be legally bound hereby, do promise and agree as follows:

1. License Grant
   A. OWNER hereby grants to COMPANY, for the Term of this Agreement, the exclusive right and license to create, develop, use, manufacture, have manufactured, sell, distribute, and advertise the Licensed Product in the countries identified in Schedule A attached hereto (the "Licensed Territory"). The license includes a license under all patents and copyrights and any applications therefore with respect to the Property. The parties recognize that COMPANY will utilize a mark other than OWNER's mark **[name]** in conjunction with such Licensed Product.

   B. It is understood and agreed that OWNER shall retain all entertainment, merchandising, and ancillary product licensing rights not otherwise conveyed herein to the original Property. It is further understood and agreed, however, that any entertainment, merchandising, and ancillary product licensing rights associated with the Licensed Product and/or any mark utilized by COMPANY in conjunction therewith will be the sole and exclusive property of COMPANY provided, however, that OWNER shall be entitled to receive a portion of the income derived by COMPANY from the commercialization of such rights as specified herein.

C. COMPANY shall also have the right to grant sublicenses to third parties to manufacture and/or sell the Licensed Product in countries in the Licensed Territory other than the United States subject to OWNER's prior express written approval of each such sublicense.

D. COMPANY shall also have the absolute, unfettered right to grant licenses to third parties to exploit the entertainment, merchandising, and ancillary product licensing rights in the Licensed Product.

E. COMPANY shall not make, use, or sell the Licensed Product or any products which are confusingly or substantially similar thereto in any country outside the Licensed Territory, and will not knowingly sell the Licensed Product to persons who intend to or are likely to resell them in a country outside the Licensed Territory.

2. Term

This Agreement shall be effective as of the date of execution by both parties and shall extend for as long as COMPANY or its sublicensee or distributors continue to manufacture or sell the Licensed Product ("Term").

3. Compensation

A. In consideration for the licenses granted hereunder, COMPANY agrees to pay OWNER the royalty recited in Schedule A (the "Royalty") based on COMPANY's Net Sales of the Licensed Product.

B. Should COMPANY grant any approved sublicenses in countries outside the United States to distribute or sell the Licensed Product, COMPANY shall pay OWNER **[number]** Percent (___%) of the gross income received by COMPANY from such sublicensees.

C. Should COMPANY grant any licenses to third parties to exploit or commercialize COMPANY's entertainment, merchandising, or ancillary product licensing rights, COMPANY agrees to pay OWNER **[number]** Percent (___%) of the total income that it receives from such licensees.

D. The Royalty owed OWNER shall be calculated on a quarterly calendar basis ("Royalty Period") and shall be payable no later than **[number]** days after the termination of the preceding full calendar quarter, i.e., commencing on the first (1st) day of January, April, July, and October, except that the first and last calendar quarters may be "short" depending on the effective date of this Agreement.

E. For each Royalty Period, COMPANY shall provide OWNER with a written royalty statement in a form acceptable to OWNER. Such royalty statement shall be certified as accurate by a duly authorized officer of COMPANY reciting, on a country-by-country basis, the stock number, item, units sold, description, quantity shipped, gross invoice, amount billed customers less discounts, allowances, returns, and reportable sales for each Licensed Product. Such statements shall be furnished to OWNER regardless of whether any Licensed Products were sold during the Royalty Period or whether any actual Royalty was owed.

F. COMPANY agrees to pay OWNER an Advance against Royalties in the amount recited in Schedule A which may be credited against COMPANY's actual royalty obligation to OWNER.

G. "Net Sales" shall mean Licensee's gross sales (the gross invoice amount billed customers) of Licensed Products, less taxes, shipping charges, quantity trade discounts actually shown on the invoice and, further, less any *bona fide* returns (net of all returns actually made or allowed as supported by credit memoranda actually issued to the customers). In no event may the total credit taken by Licensee for all discounts and returns taken during any Royalty Period exceed **[number]** Percent (___ %) of the gross sales of Licensed Products for such Royalty Period. No credit will be permitted for cash or early payment discounts or allowances. No other costs incurred in the manufacturing, selling, advertising, and distribution of the Licensed Products shall be deducted nor shall any deduction be allowed for any uncollectible accounts or allowances.

I. A Royalty obligation shall accrue upon the sale of the Licensed Product regardless of the time of collection by COMPANY. A Licensed Product shall be considered "sold" when such Licensed Product is billed, invoiced, shipped, or paid for, whichever occurs first.

J. If COMPANY sells any Licensed Product to any affiliated or related party at a price less than the regular price charged to other parties, the Royalty shall be computed at the regular price.

K. The receipt or acceptance by OWNER of any royalty statement or payment shall not prevent OWNER from subsequently challenging the validity or accuracy of such statement or payment.

L. Upon expiration or termination of this Agreement, all Royalty obligations, including the Guaranteed Minimum Royalty, shall be accelerated and shall immediately become due and payable.

M. COMPANY's obligations for the payment of Royalties shall survive expiration or termination of this Agreement, and will continue for so long as COMPANY continues to sell the Licensed Product.

N. All payments due OWNER shall be made in U.S. currency by check drawn on a U.S. bank, unless otherwise specified by OWNER.

O. Late payments shall incur interest at the rate of **[number]** Percent (__%) per month from the date such payments were originally due.

4. Record Inspection and Audit

A. OWNER shall have the right, upon reasonable notice, to inspect COMPANY's books and records and all other documents and material in COMPANY's possession or control with respect to the subject matter of this Agreement. OWNER shall have free and full access thereto for such purposes and may make copies thereof.

B. In the event that such inspection reveals an underpayment by COMPANY of the actual Royalty owed OWNER, COMPANY shall pay the difference, plus interest calculated at the rate of **[number]** Percent (__%) per month. If such underpayment be in excess of **[number]** U.S. Dollars ($ __) for any Royalty Period, COMPANY shall also reimburse OWNER for the cost of such inspection.

C. All books and records relative to COMPANY's obligations hereunder shall be maintained and made accessible to OWNER for inspection at a location in the United States for at least **[number]** years after termination of this Agreement.

5. Representations, Warranties, and Obligations

A. OWNER represents and warrants that it has the right and power to grant the licenses granted herein and that there are no other agreements with any other party in conflict with such grant.

B. OWNER further represents and warrants that it has no actual knowledge that the Property as submitted to COMPANY infringes any valid rights of any third party.

C. COMPANY represents and warrants that it shall obtain all required permissions and licenses from all third parties to permit it to distribute and sell the Licensed Product;

D. COMPANY agrees to create and develop the

Licensed Product pursuant to a schedule to be agreed upon between the parties.

E. COMPANY represents and warrants that the Licensed Product shall be of the highest professional quality and shall be accomplished in compliance with all applicable laws and regulations and in accordance with any terms and conditions set forth herein.

F. COMPANY represents and warrants that it will use its best efforts to promote, market, advertise, sell, and distribute the Licensed Product in the Licensed Territory and agrees to the Advertising Commitment recited in Schedule A.

G. COMPANY shall be solely responsible for the manufacture, production, sale, and distribution of the Licensed Product and will bear all costs associated therewith.

H. COMPANY shall introduce the Licensed Product in all countries in the Licensed Territory before the Product Introduction Date recited in Schedule A and commence shipment of Licensed Product in all countries in the Licensed Territory before the Initial Shipment Date recited therein. This is a material provision of this Agreement.

6. Notices and Samples

A. COMPANY shall fully comply with the marking provisions of the intellectual property laws of the applicable countries in the Licensed Territory.

B. The Licensed Product and all promotional, packaging, and advertising material shall include all appropriate legal notices as required by OWNER.

C. The Licensed Product shall be of a high quality that is at least equal to comparable products manufactured and marketed by COMPANY and in conformity with a standard sample approved by OWNER.

D. If the quality of a class of the Licensed Products falls below such a production run quality, as previously approved by OWNER, COMPANY shall use its best efforts to restore such quality. In the event that COMPANY has not taken reasonable steps to restore such quality within **[number]** days after notification by OWNER, OWNER shall have the right to terminate this Agreement.

E. At least once during each calendar year, COMPANY shall submit to OWNER **[number]** samples of the Licensed Product for approval.

7. Intellectual Property Rights

A. All right, title, and interest in and to all text, graphics, animation, audio and/or digital video components, and all other components of the Product other than the Software, as defined below ("Content"), including without limitation, any copyrights, trade secrets, and other intellectual or industrial property rights therein, is and shall be held by COMPANY, and shall be considered "works made for hire," as that term is defined in The Copyright Act of 1976, as amended. If for any reason the Content is not deemed to be "works made for hire," OWNER hereby assigns all copyrights therein to COMPANY.

B. All right, title, and interest in and to any computer code (both source and object) including, but not limited to, all interfaces, navigational devices, menus, menu structures or arrangements, icons, help, and other operational instructions and the literal and nonliteral expressions of ideas that operate, cause, create, direct, manipulate, access, or otherwise affect the Content in the Product ("Software") including without limitation, any copyrights, trade secrets, and other intellectual or industrial property rights therein is and shall be held by OWNER, provided however, that Software shall not include Content and COMPANY property.

C. OWNER may, but is not obligated to seek, in its own name and at its own expense, appropriate patent, trademark, or copyright protection for the Property. OWNER makes no representation or warranty with respect to the validity of any patent, trademark, or copyright which may be granted with respect to the Property.

D. It is understood and agreed that OWNER, or its grantor, shall retain all right, title, and interest in the original Property although all rights in the Licensed Product, including any modifications or improvements therein, shall be the sole and exclusive property of the COMPANY.

E. Both during the Term of this Agreement and at any time thereafter, the parties agree to execute any documents reasonably requested by the other party to effect any of the above provisions.

F. COMPANY acknowledges OWNER's exclusive rights in the Property and that the Property is unique and original to OWNER and that OWNER is the owner thereof. Unless otherwise permitted by law, COMPANY shall not, at any time during or after the effective Term of the Agreement, dispute or contest, directly or indirectly, OWNER's exclusive right and title to the Property or the validity thereof.

8. Termination

The following termination rights are in addition to the termination rights which may be provided elsewhere in the Agreement:

A. Immediate Right of Termination. OWNER shall have the right to immediately terminate this Agreement by giving written notice to COMPANY in the event that COMPANY does any of the following:

1. fails to obtain or maintain product liability insurance in the amount and of the type provided for herein;

2. files a petition in bankruptcy or is adjudicated a bankrupt or insolvent, or makes an assignment for the benefit of creditors, or an arrangement pursuant to any bankruptcy law, or if COMPANY discontinues or dissolves its business or if a receiver is appointed for COMPANY or for COMPANY's business and such receiver is not discharged within **[number]** days;

3. ceases to market any Licensed Product for **[number]** consecutive Royalty Periods;

4. fails to meet the Product Introduction and First Shipment Dates provided for herein; or

5. fails to achieve a Minimum Royalty of at least **[number]** U.S. Dollars ($ ___) per year commencing in **[year]** and COMPANY fails to supplement the earned royalty payments actually made (including any advances) to achieve that Minimum Royalty figure for each year.

B. Immediate Right to Terminate a Portion. OWNER shall have the immediate right to terminate the portion of this Agreement relating to any Property, Licensed Product, and/or country in the Licensed Territory if COMPANY, for any reason, fails to meet the Product Introduction Date or the Initial Shipment Date specified in Schedule A with respect to such Property, Licensed Product or country, or after the commencement of manufacture and sale of a particular Licensed Product in a particular country, COMPANY ceases to sell commercial quantities of such Licensed Product in such country for **[number]** consecutive Royalty Periods. In such event, that Property, Licensed Product or country shall be deemed severed from the Agreement and revert to OWNER with no restrictions.

C. Right to Terminate on Notice. Either party may terminate this Agreement on **[number]** days' written notice to the other party in the event of a breach of any provision of this Agreement by the other party, provided that, during the **[number]**-day period, the breaching party fails to cure such breach.

D. COMPANY Right to Terminate. COMPANY shall have the right to terminate this Agreement at any time on **[number]** days' written notice to OWNER, such termination to become effective at the conclusion of such **[number]**-day period.

9. Post-Termination Rights

A. Not less than **[number]** days prior to the expiration of this Agreement or immediately upon termination thereof, COMPANY shall provide OWNER with a complete schedule of all inventory of Licensed Product then on-hand ("Inventory").

B. Upon expiration or termination of this Agreement, except for reason of a breach of COMPANY's duty to comply with the quality control or legal notice marking requirements, COMPANY shall be entitled, for **[number]** months ("Sell-Off Period") and on a non-exclusive basis, to continue to sell such Inventory. Such sales shall be made subject to all the provisions of this Agreement including the payment of a Royalty which shall be due within **[number]** days after the close of the Sell-Off Period. At the conclusion of the Sell-Off Period, OWNER may require that COMPANY either destroy any product still on hand or, alternatively, purchase it from COMPANY at a price equal to **[number]** Percent (___%) of COMPANY's Net Selling Price.

C. Upon the expiration or termination of this Agreement, all rights granted to COMPANY under this Agreement shall forthwith terminate and immediately revert to OWNER, and COMPANY shall discontinue all use of the Property and the like.

D. Upon expiration or termination of this Agreement, OWNER may require that COMPANY transmit to OWNER, at no cost, all material relating to the Property including all artwork, color separations, prototypes, and the like, and any market studies or other tests conducted by COMPANY with respect to the Property.

10. Infringements

A. OWNER shall have the right, in its sole discretion, to prosecute lawsuits against third persons for infringement of OWNER's rights in the Property. If OWNER does not institute an infringement suit within **[number]** days after COMPANY's written request that it do so, COMPANY may institute and prosecute such lawsuit.

B. Any lawsuit shall be prosecuted solely at the expense of the party bringing suit and all sums recovered shall be divided equally between OWNER and COMPANY after deduction of all reasonable expenses and attorney fees.

C. The parties agree to fully cooperate with the other party in the prosecution of any such suit. The party bringing suit shall reimburse the other party for the expenses incurred as a result of such cooperation.

11. Indemnity

A. COMPANY agrees to defend, indemnify, and hold OWNER, and its officers, directors, agents, and employees, harmless against all costs, expenses, and losses (including reasonable attorney fees and costs) incurred through claims of third parties against OWNER based on the manufacture or sale of the Licensed Product including, but not limited to, actions founded on product liability.

B. OWNER agrees to defend, indemnify, and hold COMPANY, and its officers, directors, agents, and employees, harmless against all costs, expenses, and losses (including reasonable attorney fees and costs) incurred through claims of third parties against COMPANY based on a breach by OWNER of any representation and warranty made in this Agreement.

12. Insurance

COMPANY shall, throughout the Term of the Agreement, obtain and maintain at its own cost and expense from a qualified insurance company licensed to do business in **[state]** with a Moody's Rating of B+ or better, standard Product Liability Insurance naming OWNER, its officers, directors, employees, agents, and shareholders as an additional insured. Such policy shall provide protection against all claims, demands, and causes of action arising out of any defects or failure to perform, alleged or otherwise, of the Licensed Product or any material used in connection therewith or any use thereof. The amount of coverage shall be as specified in Schedule A attached hereto. The policy shall provide for **[number]** days' notice to OWNER from the insurer by registered or certified mail, return receipt requested, in the event of any modification, cancellation, or termination thereof. COMPANY agrees to furnish OWNER a certificate of insurance evidencing same within **[number]** days after execution of this Agreement and, in no event shall COMPANY manufacture, distribute, or sell the Licensed Product prior to receipt by OWNER of such evidence of insurance.

13. Force Majeure

Neither party shall be liable for any loss or delay resulting from any force majeure event, including acts of God, fire, natural disaster, labor stoppage, war or military hostilities, or inability of carriers to make scheduled deliveries, and any payment or delivery date shall be extended to the extent of any delay resulting from any force majeure event.

14. Notices

A. Any notice required to be given pursuant to this Agreement shall be in writing and mailed by certified or registered mail, return receipt requested, or delivered by a national overnight express service.

B. Either party may change the address to which notice or payment is to be sent by written notice to the other party pursuant to the provisions of this paragraph.

15. Jurisdiction and Disputes

A. This Agreement shall be governed by the laws of **[state]**.

B. All disputes hereunder shall be resolved in the applicable state or federal courts of **[state]**. The parties consent to the jurisdiction of such courts, agree to accept service of process by mail, and waive any jurisdictional or venue defenses otherwise available.

16. Agreement Binding on Successors

This Agreement shall be binding upon and shall inure to the benefit of the parties hereto, and their heirs, administrators, successors, and assigns.

17. Waiver

No waiver by either party of any default shall be deemed as a waiver of any prior or subsequent default of the same or other provisions of this Agreement.

18. Severability

If any provision hereof is held invalid or unenforceable by a court of competent jurisdiction, such invalidity shall not affect the validity or operation of any other provision and such invalid provision shall be deemed to be severed from the Agreement.

19. Assignability

The license granted hereunder is personal to COMPANY and may not be assigned by any act of COMPANY or by operation of law unless in connection with a transfer of substantially all the assets of COMPANY or with the consent of OWNER.

20. Integration

This Agreement constitutes the entire understanding of the parties, and revokes and supersedes all prior agreements between the parties and is intended as a final expression of their Agreement. It shall not be modified or amended except in writing signed by the parties hereto and specifically referring to this Agreement. This Agreement shall take precedence over any other documents which may be in conflict therewith.

IN WITNESS WHEREOF, the parties hereto have executed this Agreement as of the date first written above.

[name of OWNER]	[name of COMPANY]
By: _____	By: _____
Title: _____	Title: _____
Date: _____	Date: _____

SCHEDULE A

1. Property

The Property is identified in the attached Exhibit A.

2. Licensed Products

The Licensed Products are as follows: **[specify type of product, e.g., Interactive, multimedia video game]**.

3. Licensed Territory

The following countries shall constitute the Licensed Territory: **[specify territory, e.g., Worldwide]**

4. Royalty Rate

The Royalty Rate for both domestic and FOB sales is as follows: **[number]** Percent (___%).

5. Advance

The following Advance shall be paid upon execution of this Agreement: **[number]** U.S. Dollars ($ ___).

6. Product Liability Insurance

[Number] Dollars ($___) combined single limit, with a deductible amount not to exceed **[number]** Dollars ($___), for each single occurrence for bodily injury and/or for property damage.

7. Product Introduction/Initial Shipment

The Product Introduction Date for all Licensed Products in the United States shall be the **[specify event and location, e.g., Comdex Show in Las Vegas]** in **[year]**.

The Initial Shipment Date for all Licensed Products in the United States shall be **[date]**.

The Product Introduction Date and Initial Shipment Date for all other countries shall be **[number]** year after the applicable date in the United States.

8. Advertising Commitment

Commencing in **[year]**, OWNER agrees to expend at least **[number]** Dollars ($___) in media placements in order to advertise the Licensed Product.

Exhibit A

[Attach Sample of Property]

Index

-A-

Advances against royalties, 111
Agents, 14-15
American Arbitration Association (AAA), 121-122
Anti-dilution protection, 36
Antitrust Guidelines, revised 130-131
Apple Computer, 3-4
Arbitration, 121-122
Assignments, 102, 122-123
Audits, 113-114, 166-175

-B-

Benefits of licensing, 2-5
Biotechnology, 177-184
Block exemptions, 150-153
Borchard, Bill, 24
Brenner, Dan, 189
Budgeting, 12-13
Bureau of Export Administration, 138

-C-

China, People's Republic of, 156-159
Clayton Act, 126
Common law protection, 36
Comparability (intellectual property), 57
Computer industry, 186-187
Confidential disclosure agreements, 90-93, 203
Consultancy agreement, sample, 209-218
Consultants, 15, 20, 196-202
Contact list, 85
Copyright, 10, 25, 32-35
Court of Appeals for the Federal Circuit (CAFC), 71
Cross-licensing, 6
Current assets, 44
Current liabilities, 44

-D-

Damages, infringement, 71-73, 77-82
Department of Justice (DOJ), 128-129
Design patents, 26, 39

Determining royalty rates, 61-64
Dilution, 36
Disputes, 121-122

-E-
European Economic Community (EEC), 149-153
European Trademark Office (EPO), 41
Evaluation periods, 95-97
Evans, Larry, 157
Excess earnings, 48-49
Exclusivity, defined, 103
Export Administration Act of 1979, 138

-F-
Favored nation clauses, 106, 118
Federal Trade Commission (FTC), 86, 126, 130
Five percent sales method, 69-70
Fixed assets, 44
Foreign currency, 146-148
Foreign export controls, 138

-G-
Gate keeper, 87
Georgia-Pacific, 77-82
Goldscheider, Robert, 164
Grant-backs, 115-116
Guaranteed minimum royalties, 111

-I-
IBM, 3-4
Improvements, 115-116
Indemnification, 7, 118-119
Industry norms method, 67
Intangible assets, 45
Integration, 123
Intellectual property laws, 23-41
Interactive multimedia, 187-188
Invention companies, 86
Invention Secrecy Act, 139
Investigation, royalty, 169-175

-J-
Jacobson, Dan, 171-172
Japan, 154-156
Joint ventures, 90, 102, 127, 180

-L-

Lanham Act, 32, 36
Letter of intent, 103-106
Licensed property, defined, 1, 108
licensee, defined, 1, 107
Licensing Economics Review (LER), 43, 195
Licensing Executives Society (LES), 15, 20, 193
Licensing in, 5, 17-21
Licensing Journal, The, 171, 195
Licensing out, 6, 9-17
Licensor, defined, 1, 107
Litigation, 117, 122

-M-

Maintenance fees, patents, 29
Marketing plans, elements of, 13
Memorandum, licensing, 87, 88-90
Microsoft, 128-129
Misuse, patent, 132-135
Mogen David, 30, 39
Multimedia, 185-191
Multimedia license agreement, sample, 268-286

-N-

National Cable Television Association, 189
Net sales definition, 113
NEXIS, 85
Non-exclusivity, 103
Normal industry profit margins, 74
Notices, legal, 39-40

-O-

Office Actions, 28
Office of Defense Trade Controls (ODTC), 139
Option agreements, 97-99, 219-220
Options to renew, 108-109
Overlapping intellectual property protection, 37-39

-P-

Pacific Rim, 153-161
Paid-up licenses, 110
Parr, Russell, L. 43, 194-195
Patent license agreement, sample, 221-251
Patent pending, 27, 40
Patents, 26-29
Plant patents, 26-27

Product liability exposure, 7
Public domain, 2

-Q-
Quality control, 7

-R-
R&D costs, 68-69
Recordation requirements, 145
Renewal options, 108-109
Return on sales, 69
Risks of licensing, 6-8
Royalty, defined, 2

-S-
Secondary meaning, 37
Sherman Act, 125
Shortened statutory period, 28
South Korea, 159-161
Sublicensing, 112-113, 122

-T-
Technology license agreement, sample, 252-267
Term of license, 108
Termination, 119
Territory, 108

Trade secret protection, 25
Trademark licensing, 7
Trademarks, 29-32
Treaty of Rome, 149, 153
Twenty-five percent rule, 65-67
TX, Copyright Form, 34

-U-
Unfair competition, 35
Utility patents, 26

-V-
VA, Copyright Form, 34
Virtual reality, 188-189

-W-
Waiver agreements, 91-92
Warranties, 7, 118-119
Working capital, 44
Works for hire, 35, 38